BURNS
COUNTRY

DAVID CARROLL

The
History
Press

For Ernie Smith –
a keen Burnsian

First published 1999
This edition first published 2009

The History Press
The Mill, Brimscombe Port
Stroud, Gloucestershire, GL5 2QG
www.thehistorypress.co.uk

© David Carroll 1999, 2009

The right of David Carroll to be identified as the Author
of this work has been asserted in accordance with the
Copyrights, Designs and Patents Act 1988.

British Library Cataloguing in Publication Data.
A catalogue record for this book is available from the British Library.

ISBN 978 0 7524 4956 2

Typesetting and origination by The History Press
Printed in Great Britain

Cover illustrations: Portrait of Robert Burns taken from a picture postcard
and 1930s' tourist postcard view of Moffatdale

CONTENTS

The High Parish Kirk, Kilmarnock, *c.* 1905. John Wilson, from whose printing press tumbled the first edition of Burns's *Poems, Chiefly in the Scottish Dialect*, is buried in the kirkyard here.

INTRODUCTION

'**B**urns's country was the Western Lowlands of Scotland' declared the poet Edward Thomas in an essay written just before the outbreak of the First World War. 'The poor, free peasantry culminated in him. Poetry does not sum up, but his poetry was the flower and essence of that country and its peasantry. He was great', Thomas emphasized, 'because they were all at his back, their life and their literature.'

'Burns Country' could probably best be defined in more specific terms as those parts of the old county of Ayrshire and the present region of Dumfries and Galloway where Burns was born, lived, laboured and developed into Scotland's national poet. Many literary visitors have recorded their impressions of Burns's native country over the years but perhaps one of the most pleasing descriptions comes from the pen of John Keats, a poet whose genius – like that of Burns's own – was extinguished by an early death. Approaching Alloway in July 1818, 'I had no conception that the native place of Burns was so beautiful,' Keats exploded, 'the idea I had was more desolate. His "rigs of barley" seemed always to me but a few strips of green on a cold hill. O prejudice! It was as rich as Devon. . . . We came down upon everything suddenly: there were in our way the "bonny Doon", with the brig that "Tam o' Shanter" crossed, Kirk Alloway, Burns's cottage and the Brigs o' Ayr. First we stood upon the bridge across the Doon', related Keats, who was travelling with his friend Charles Brown, 'surrounded by every phantasy of green in tree, meadow and hill; the stream of the Doon, as a farmer told us, is covered with trees "from head to foot" – you know those beautiful heaths so fresh against the weather of a summer's evening – there was one stretching along behind the trees.'

However, Keats's evocation of this pastoral idyll should not be allowed to blind us to the fact that Burns grew up – at Alloway, then later at Mount Oliphant and Lochlea – in conditions of considerable hardship. The poet's brother Gilbert, recalling these early times, explained that the family 'lived very sparingly. For several years butcher's meat was a stranger in the house, while all the members of the family exerted themselves to the utmost of their strength, and rather beyond it, in the labours of the farm. . . .'

Burns died long before photography became the universal means by which we are able to capture a scene for the benefit of posterity. To discover how 'Burns Country' might have appeared in the poet's own time – the second half of the eighteenth century – we have to rely upon the occasional artist's (often highly idealized) impression of a building, town, village or sweep of landscape, or perhaps on a scrap of contemporary written description. If we are particularly fortunate, remnants of that bygone age – the birthplace cottage at Alloway, for example, or the poet's last home in Dumfries – will have been handed down to us, often much changed in the intervening years but just as likely to have been restored by now to something exceeding their original glory; one of the beneficial effects of our late twentieth-century preoccupation with the past.

Even the earliest photograph to appear in this volume was not taken until more than sixty years after Burns's death but I hope that this present selection, drawn almost entirely from the albums of private collectors who are themselves resident in 'Burns Country', serves to provide a comprehensive and illuminating backdrop to the region in which Burns spent his brief life as labourer, ploughman, farmer, Exciseman and – above all – poet.

Every effort has been made to verify the dates and information given in the text. Also, every attempt has been made to trace the copyright holders of photographs wherever this was appropriate. I can only apologize for any unintentional omissions, which I would be pleased to rectify upon notification in any future edition of this work.

Among the many people who helped me in various ways during the preparation of this book, I am particularly grateful to Ian Ball for giving me unrestricted access to his postcard collection and for devoting so much time to combing through the photographs in his care; to Ernie Smith for his generous and tireless assistance in locating photographs and researching their contents on my behalf; and to Richard Stenlake for delving into his postcard collection and providing me with so many useful images of 'Burns Country'.

Burns Country would certainly have proved more difficult to compile than was actually the case were it not for the earlier exertions of two authors, Andrew Boyle and James A. Mackay, whose *Ayrshire Book of Burns-Lore* and *Burns-Lore of Dumfries and Galloway* respectively (both from Alloway Publishing Ltd) are essential reference tools for anyone attempting to explore the connection between Burns and the landscape in which he lived, worked and generally had his being.

Finally, I must thank Bernadette Walsh for helping to select and arrange the photographs in this volume.

David Carroll
Shieldhill, Dumfriesshire, 1999

CHAPTER ONE
AROUND ALLOWAY & AYR

The long, low cottage where Robert Burns was born in January 1759 is pictured above during the 1930s. Once situated in the separate village of Alloway, the 'auld clay biggin' with its thatched roof and whitewashed walls now stands on the southern fringe of Ayr. The dwelling was built by Burns's father in 1756 using, as the present-day Scottish poet Douglas Dunn points out, materials 'with which Burns struggled for so much of his relatively short life – clay, earth, dirt, ground'. (See Kate March (ed.) *Writers and their Houses*, 1993). Burns lived here until he was seven, when his family moved to nearby Mount Oliphant. Subsequently the cottage served as an alehouse (John Keats drank Toddy here in July 1818 during a walking tour of the area), and it is in this guise that the cottage is seen below in 1862. The property was then owned by the Ayr Corporation of Shoemakers, but in 1881 it was acquired by the Alloway Burns Monument Trustees for £4,000. Over the next twenty years the building was thoroughly renovated, and it opened in March 1901 as the Burns Cottage and Museum that we are familiar with today, and which attracts an endless stream of the poet's admirers from all over the world.

This somewhat idealized impression of early nineteenth-century Alloway, and the cottage where Burns first saw the light of day, is by the Scottish photographer and painter David Octavius Hill, *c.* 1840. The first Burns Supper – or, at least, the first one that we know about and a forerunner of the many thousands that have since followed worldwide – was held at the poet's birthplace in 1801 (although, unlike nowadays, it did not coincide with Burns's birthday at the end of January). History records that the evening included a rendering of the 'Address to a Haggis' which, according to a report in the *Edinburgh Literary Journal* in 1829, was composed at the home of a Mauchline cabinetmaker. '[Morrison] was a great crony of Burns's,' the writer explained, 'and it was [at his home] that the poet usually spent the "mids o' the day" on Sunday. It was in this house that he wrote the celebrated "Address to a Haggis" after partaking liberally of that dish as prepared by Mrs Morrison.' However, there seems to be some doubt as to whether or not this was actually the case. Maurice Lindsay, writing in *The Burns Encyclopedia* (1980 edn), points out that the poem may have been composed in Edinburgh in 1786, at the home of the poet's friend Andrew Bruce.

> Fair fa' your honest, sonsie face,
> Great chieftain o' the puddin-race!
> Aboon them a' ye tak your place,
>   Painch, tripe or thairm:
> Weel are ye wordy o' a grace
>   As lang's my arm.
>
> Ye Pow'rs wha mak mankind your care,
> And dish them out their bill o' fare,
> Auld Scotland wants nae skinking ware
>   That jaups in luggies;
> But, if ye wish her gratefu' prayer
>   Gie her a Haggis!

Two views showing the interior of Burns Cottage (named New Gardens by the poet's father) at Alloway. Everything is cleared up and tidied away here, of course, in readiness for visitors. It was a typical farmhouse of its period, fairly dark and probably cramped but with the advantage (not universal at the time) that humans and animals occupied separate quarters. Recalling his childhood, Burns wrote:

> There, lanely, by the ingle cheek,
> I sat and ey'd the spewing reek,
> That fill'd, wi' hoast-provoking smeek
>   The auld clay biggin;
> And heard the restless rattons squeak
>   About the riggin.

The Auld Brig o' Doon, Alloway, 1950s. Spanning the River Doon, the single-arched bridge (now only open to pedestrians) is at least 500 years old and quite possibly of an earlier vintage. A modern bridge nearby carries motorized traffic. Unremarkable though it may appear to the layman, the bridge is one of the great landmarks in 'Burns Country'. Famous throughout the world, it is immortalized in the climax of 'Tam o' Shanter' as the spot where Tam's mare Meg lost her tail to the witch Nannie:

> Now, do thy speedy utmost, Meg,
> And win the key-stane o' the brig;
> There, at them thou thy tail may toss,
> A running stream they dare na cross.
> But ere the key-stane she could make,
> The fient a tail she had to shake!
> For Nannie, far before the rest,
> Hard upon noble Maggie prest,
> And flew at Tam with furious ettle;
> But little wist she Maggie's mettle!
> Ae spring brought off her master hale,
> But left behind her ain grey tail:
> The carlin claught her by the rump,
> And left poor Maggie scarce a stump.

Auld Alloway Kirk (or Kirk-Alloway), *c.* 1910. Built in the early sixteenth century but no more than a ruin during Burns's childhood, it appears in 'Tam o' Shanter' as the setting for the witches' dance:

> Kirk-Alloway seem'd in a bleeze,
> Thro' ilka bore the beams were glancing,
> And loud resounded mirth and dancing.

The poet's father and youngest sister are buried in the kirkyard.

A timeless scene and one that has graced many a calendar over the years, as sunset bathes the Ayrshire coast in evening light at Ayr, 1937. This beautiful stretch of coastline, looking across the Firth of Clyde towards the Isle of Arran, was at one time a favourite holiday haunt for people who lived and worked in the Clydeside shipbuilding towns. Earlier it had formed an integral part of Burns's personal landscape; a spot that was familiar to him not only while living and growing up around Ayr, but one that he would have revisited in his mind's eye throughout his life.

The Twa Brigs, Ayr, early 1900s. These two bridges set close together span the River Ayr where it passes through the centre of this bustling coastal town. The Auld Brig (which is now only open to pedestrians) dates from the thirteenth century and was restored in 1910. Burns's poem 'The Brigs of Ayr' was written in 1786 when building work was begun on an adjacent new bridge. It was opened two years later, but this structure was destroyed by flooding in 1877 and so another new bridge (pictured here in the foreground) was erected the following year. Much emphasis is always placed on the fact that in his poem (which takes the form of an imaginary conversation between the pair of bridges) Burns seemed to prophesy the premature demise of the 'upstart rival':

> Conceited gowk! puff'd up wi' windy pride!
> [the Auld Brig declares],
> This mony a year I've stood the flood an' tide;
> And tho' wi' crazy eild I'm sair forfairn,
> I'll be a brig when ye're a shapeless cairn!
>
> . . .
>
> When heavy, dark, continued a'-day rains,
> Wi' deepening deluges o'erflow the plains;
> When from the hills where springs the brawling Coil,
> Or stately Lugar's mossy fountains boil;
>
> . . .
>
> Then down ye'll hurl (deil nor ye never rise!)
> And dash the gumlie jaups up to the pouring skies!
> A lesson sadly teaching, to your cost,
> That Architecture's noble art is lost!

Stepping stones reach across a quiet stretch of the River Ayr, 1920s. Burns was closely acquainted with much of the river's 30-odd miles' course and was sentimentally attached to it throughout his life. There was a period during 1786 when the poet might have emigrated to Jamaica and left his native land for good. Those plans were later abandoned, but not before he had composed 'Farewell to the Banks of Ayr':

The gloomy night is gath'ring fast,
Loud roars the wild, inconstant blast,
Yon murky cloud is foul with rain,
I see it driving o'er the plain;
The hunter now has left the moor,
The scatt'red coveys meet secure;
While here I wander, prest with care,
Along the lonely banks of Ayr.

. . .

Farewell, old Coila's hills and dales,
Her heathy moors and winding vales;
The scenes where wretched Fancy roves,
Pursuing past, unhappy loves!
Farewell, my friends! farewell, my foes!
My peace with these, my love with those:
The bursting tears my heart declare –
Farewell, the bonie banks of Ayr!

The Harbour, Ayr, probably late nineteenth century. 'Auld Ayr, whom ne'er a town surpasses,/For honest men and bonie lasses,' wrote Burns in 'Tam o' Shanter'.

Sandgate, Ayr, early 1900s. John Murdoch, who taught the young Burns at Alloway when still only in his late teens himself, lived in this thoroughfare after becoming an English master at Ayr Grammar School some years later. Burns attended the Grammar School for a few weeks in 1773 while Murdoch was in post, and lodged at his former teacher's house. Given the nature of Burns's subsequent career and achievements, Murdoch has left a surprising impression of the poet in his early years. From a musical point of view, he recalled: 'Robert's ear was remarkably dull and his voice untunable. It was long before I could get [him] to distinguish one tune from another.'

Two views of High Street, Ayr: looking north, *c.* 1903 (above) and looking south, *c.* 1939 (below), with the Wallace Tower presiding over the scene in each case. The 113 ft high Gothic tower pictured here dates from 1834 (and was thus erected long after Burns's time), but it stands on the site of an ancient predecessor. Burns refers to the old tower in 'The Brigs of Ayr':

The drowsy Dungeon-clock had number'd two,
And Wallace Tower had sworn the fact was true. . . .

Doonfoot, Ayr, where the River Doon enters the sea, 1930s. This stretch of the river would have been a familiar sight to the young Burns while he was growing up in the cottage at Alloway and, later, at Mount Oliphant, so it is hardly surprising that references to the River Doon often crop up in his work. 'The Banks o' Doon' is among the poet's most popular songs:

> Ye banks and braes o' bonie Doon,
> How can ye bloom sae fresh and fair?
> How can ye chant, ye little birds,
> And I sae weary fu' o' care?
> Thou'll break my heart, thou warbling bird,
> That wantons thro' the flowering thorn:
> Thou minds me o' departed joys,
> Departed never to return.
>
> Aft hae I rov'd by bonie Doon,
> To see the rose and woodbine twine;
> And ilka bird sang o' its Luve,
> And fondly sae did I o' mine;
> Wi' lightsome heart I pu'd a rose,
> Fu' sweet upon its thorny tree!
> And my fause Luver staw my rose
> But ah! he left the thorn wi' me.

The Auld Kirk, Ayr, *c.* 1912. As a boy Burns worshipped here with his parents, and a number of people who were later associated with the poet are buried in the kirkyard, including Robert Aiken to whom Burns dedicated 'The Cottar's Saturday Night' and who also earns a mention in 'Holy Willie's Prayer', 'The Farewell' and 'The Kirk's Alarm'. The church was built in the mid-seventeenth century with compensation money provided by Oliver Cromwell. Cromwell's army had taken over the town's twelfth-century Church of St John and incorporated it into a fort.

Belleisle House, Ayr, 1930s. In more recent years this building has served as a hotel but, as James A. Mackay points out in his *Land o' Burns* (1996), the Glentanar family (whose home this was in former times) filled the main hallway with Burns-related figures, friezes and bas-reliefs, all of which were executed by Italian craftsmen. Scenes from 'Tam o' Shanter', 'The Jolly Beggars' and 'Death and Dr Hornbook' are among those that greet guests on their arrival at Belleisle House.

CHAPTER TWO
AROUND MOUNT OLIPHANT & LOCHLEA

Mount Oliphant, pictured during the late nineteenth century (above) and 1930s/40s (below). Burns was seven when he moved with his family to this farm south-east of Alloway in 1766. It was about 70 acres in size but the land was very poor, and simply trying to make ends meet proved extremely difficult, but the family struggled on here until 1777. The poet's brother Gilbert wrote later that 'at the age of thirteen [Robert] assisted in threshing the crop of corn, and at fifteen was the principal labourer of the farm. . . . I doubt not but the hard labour and sorrow of this period of his life was in great measure the cause of that depression of spirits with which Robert was so often afflicted through his whole life afterwards.' On the brighter side, however, Burns composed his first known song while living at Mount Oliphant. In 1773, aged fourteen and inspired by Nelly Kilpatrick, who was the boy's companion in the harvest field that autumn, Burns wrote the words of 'Handsome Nell'. Recalling that time in his *First Commonplace Book* ten years later, he explained that 'I never had the least thought or inclination of turning poet till I got once heartily in love, and then rhyme and song were, in a manner, the spontaneous language of my heart.'

Kirkoswald, where Burns briefly attended school in 1775 under the tutelage of Hugh Rodger. This photograph was taken on 29 June 1929, the day that a bronze tablet was unveiled to mark the site of the school. A substantial crowd can be seen gathered outside the building in question, which later became part of the Shanter Hotel in the village's Main Street. The village kirkyard contains the headstones of Douglas Graham (the model for 'Tam o' Shanter'), John Davidson ('Souter Johnie' of 'Tam o' Shanter'), Hugh Rodger and some of Burns's relations on his mother's side.

Gardens at the rear of Hugh Rodger's school in Kirkoswald, 1920s. Burns was sixteen when he spent a term here learning what he described as mensuration, surveying and dialling. On 23 August 1775 Burns stepped out into the garden behind the school and prepared to take the altitude of the sun. He was deflected from his aim, however, by the appearance in her own garden of Peggy Thomson, the girl who lived next door. In a letter written twelve years later, Burns described her as 'a charming fillette, who . . . over-set my trigonometry and set me off in a tangent from the sphere of my studies'.

The Ladies' (or Leddies') House, Kirkoswald. The building, which had been turned into a smithy by the time this photograph was taken in the early 1900s, no longer exists. In 1775, however, when Burns was attending Hugh Rodger's school in the village, these premises served as an alehouse presided over by two sisters, Jean and Anne Kennedy. Hence its nickname The Ladies' House, which Burns slightly altered to The Lord's House when referring to it in 'Tam o' Shanter' (with Jean Kennedy herself making a brief appearance as 'Kirkton Jean').

The Bachelors' Club in Sandgate, Tarbolton, 1961. It was in this building on 4 July 1781 that Burns began his connection with Freemasonry. It was also here that, in November of the previous year, Burns and his brother Gilbert were among the founding members of a men-only debating society known as the Tarbolton Bachelors' Club (an alehouse occupied the premises in those days). One of the club's rules (which gives a fair flavour of the qualities required in its members) decreed that 'every man proper for a member of this Society must have a frank, honest, open heart; above anything dirty or mean; and must be a professed lover of one or more of the female sex. No haughty, self-conceited person, who looks upon himself as superior to the rest of the Club, and especially no mean-spirited, worldly mortal, whose only will is to heap up money shall upon any pretence whatever be admitted.' Subjects held up for discussion at the club's monthly meetings included 'Whether we derive more happiness from friendship or love' and 'Whether the savage or the peasant in a civilized country is in the most happy condition'. The building was bought by the National Trust for Scotland just before the Second World War, and nowadays it houses a museum of Burns-related relics.

Opposite: The heckling house (or shed) in the Glasgow Vennel at Irvine, where Burns went in 1781 to learn the trade of flax-dressing. The experience was not an altogether happy one, and Burns returned home to Lochlea after six months or so. 'My partner was a scoundrel of the first water,' he explained, 'who made money by the mystery of thieving; and to finish the whole, while we were giving a carousel to the new year, our shop burnt to ashes and left me, like a true poet, not worth a sixpence.'

Two early impressions of Lochlea Farm north-east of Tarbolton, which was Burns's home for seven years from 1777. (The name appeared as Lochlie in the poet's day.) The engraving below was made by E. Benjamin from a sepia drawing attributed to William Bartlett and published in 1839. Lochlea is recalled in 'The Death and Dying Words of Poor Mailie', as Gilbert Burns explained. 'Robert had partly by way of frolic bought a ewe and two lambs from a neighbour,' he wrote, 'and she was tethered in a field adjoining the house at Lochlie. He and I were going out with our teams . . . at midday when Hugh Wilson, a curious-looking boy clad in plaidings, came to us with much anxiety in his face, with the information that the ewe had entangled herself in the tether and was lying in the ditch. Robert was much tickled at the ewe's appearance and postures on the occasion. Poor Mailie was set to rights and, when we returned from the plough in the evening, he repeated to me the "Death and Dying Words", pretty much in the way they now stand.' It was at Lochlea that the poet's father William died in February 1784. The family moved to Mossgiel the following month.

Two views of Tarbolton, *c*. 1906–7. In the above photograph, showing the north side of Cunningham Street, the two-storeyed house beyond the Burns Tavern belonged to the Tarbolton schoolmaster John Wilson, who Burns immortalized as Doctor Hornbook in 'Death and Doctor Hornbook'. Wilson left Tarbolton in 1792 and went back to Glasgow (the city of his childhood) where he taught in Buchan Street. Sandgate and the south side of Cunningham Street are pictured below, with the Bachelors' Club building shown on the near left and the Cross Keys Inn beyond. John Wilson's school also stood on this side of the street but, like the Cross Keys (where Burns attended Masonic meetings), it no longer exists.

A scene from 'Death and Doctor Hornbook', illustrated by J.M. Wright and engraved by J. Rogers, 1839. Regarding his brother's inspiration for the poem, Gilbert Burns tells us that Wilson 'to eke out [his] scanty subsistence . . . set up a shop of grocery goods. Having accidentally fallen in with some medical books . . . he had added the sale of a few medicines to his little store. He had got a shop bill printed, and overlooking his own incapacity he had advertised that advice would be given in common disorders, at the shop. Robert was at a Mason-meeting at Tarbolton, when the dominie made a too ostentatious display of his medical skill.'

Burns's Street, Tarbolton, with the Burns Tavern on the near left, c. 1912. Tibbie Stein's house once stood at the far end of this street on the left-hand side (opposite Manson's Inn – now also gone). The girl's real name was Isabella Steven, although she was known locally as Tibbie Stein. She became the object of Burns's affections when he was about eighteen and living nearby at Lochlea. He is said to have composed the lines of the song 'O Tibbie, I hae seen the day' after their brief relationship had come to an end.

Willie's Mill, Tarbolton, *c.* 1900 (above) and *c.* 1910 (below). Properly called Tarbolton Mill, it was owned by Burns's friend William Muir who became the subject of a laudatory epitaph:

> An honest man here lies at rest,
> As e'er God with his image blest;
> The friend of man, the friend of truth,
> The friend of age, and guide of youth;
> Few hearts like his – with virtue warm'd,
> Few heads with knowledge so informed:
> If there's another world, he lives in bliss;
> If there is none, he made the best of this.

Manson's Inn, Tarbolton, *c.* 1900 (above), and a rear view of the premises dating from the late nineteenth century (below). The inn, which stood opposite Tibbie Stein's house, was named after its landlord James Manson. Burns, who had become a Freemason in 1781, was elected Depute Master of Lodge St James Tarbolton (which Manson served as treasurer) during a meeting held at the inn on 27 July 1784. The Lodge met at Manson's and, because he provided his fellow masons with 'small beer of a very superior kind', this led to a measure of immortality for him, after Burns referred to 'Manson's barrels' in the poem 'To Doctor John Mackenzie'.

CHAPTER THREE
AROUND MOSSGIEL

An early painting of Mossgiel near Mauchline, the property where Burns and his brother Gilbert began farming on their own in 1784. Several farms in the area bore that name, but East Mossgiel where Burns spent four years still exists today, although altered out of all recognition from the poet's time. Mossgiel is where Burns the poet flourished, and where he was living when the Kilmarnock edition of his *Poems, Chiefly in the Scottish Dialect* appeared. A ploughing match attended by 8,000 people was held at Mossgiel in 1996, one of the many events that marked the bicentenary of Burns's death.

The Cross, Mauchline, late nineteenth century. The substantial tenement building pictured on the near right-hand side and called The Place is said to have been where Mary Morison lived. Some considerable doubt exists over whether or not she was the heroine of a song that Burns composed and whose title bears her name: 'O Mary, at the window be,/It is the wish'd, the trysted hour . . .' (However, a tombstone erected in Mauchline kirkyard in 1825 declared that she was the 'poet's bonie Mary Morison'.)

Cowgate, Mauchline, early 1900s (above) and *c.* 1875 (below). The church seen here was built in 1827, many years after Burns frequented the area, and replaced its predecessor whose seventeenth-century kirkyard provided the setting for 'The Holy Fair'. Cowgate was not only an important artery leading into the village when the poet lived nearby at Mossgiel, but it was also a thoroughfare of some prominence in Burns's personal life. His wife Jean Armour lived in Cowgate with her parents prior to her marriage and – of hardly less significance – two public houses frequented by the poet could be found here. The Whitefoord Arms stood at the junction of Cowgate and Loudoun Street, and was run by John Dow or Dove ('Johnnie Doo' to his customers). The Court of Equity, described as a secret bachelors' association (Burns was its 'Perpetual President') met here 'to search out, report, and discuss the merits and demerits of the many scandals that crop up from time to time in the village . . .'. At the opposite end of Cowgate Ann Orr's alehouse provided the venue for the Mauchline Young Men's Society of which, like the Tarbolton Bachelors' Club, Burns and his brother were founder members.

Back Causeway (now called Castle Street) Mauchline, *c.* 1920. Nance Tannock's Inn (properly known as The Sma' Inn and presided over in Burns's time by Mrs Agnes Weir) is pictured on the right. The building on the near left is where Burns and Jean Armour rented rooms at the beginning of their married life. The house belonged to a local tailor called Archibald Meikle. Not surprisingly, perhaps, these premises (seen here a few years after they had been acquired on behalf of the Burns Federation) together with the house next door have been turned into the Burns House Museum.

Gavin Hamilton's house in the centre of Mauchline flanked by the church and the castle, early 1900s. A lawyer by profession and a friend and patron of the poet, Hamilton was the person to whom Burns dedicated the Kilmarnock edition of his *Poems, Chiefly in the Scottish Dialect*. It was also from Hamilton that Burns and his brother Gilbert sub-leased Mossgiel Farm (Hamilton himself leasing the property from the Earl of Loudoun). We catch a glimpse of Hamilton as seen through Burns's eyes in the poet's 'Epistle to the Rev. John M'Math':

> There's Gaw'n, misca'd waur than a beast,
> Wha has mair honor in his breast
> Than mony scores as guid's the priest
>   Wha sae abused him:
> And may a bard no crack his jest
>   What way they've us'd him!
>
> See him, the poor man's friend in need,
> The gentleman in word and deed. . . .

Opposite: This old postcard claims in its caption to show the room in Gavin Hamilton's house at Mauchline where Burns and Jean Armour were married. However, as with so many other details concerning the poet's history (not least those relating to his spectacularly chaotic love life), the truth is not as simple as that, and there has long been some confusion regarding exactly how, where and even the precise moment at which the two became one.

Two views of Loudoun Street, Mauchline, early 1900s. The Loudoun Arms Hotel pictured on the near left (below) was formerly called McLelland's Inn and was much frequented by Burns during his time at Mossgiel. The poet celebrated a select group of the town's young ladies (including the local girl who would become his wife) in 'The Belles of Mauchline':

> In Mauchline there dwells six proper young belles,
> The pride of the place and its neighbourhood a':
> Their carriage and dress, a stranger would guess,
> In London or Paris, they'd gotten it a'.
>
> Miss Miller is fine, Miss Markland's divine,
> Miss Smith she has wit, and Miss Betty is braw:
> There's beauty and fortune to get wi' Miss Morton,
> But Armour's the jewel for me o' them a'.

An impression of Poosie Nansie's Inn at the junction of Cowgate and Loudoun Street, Mauchline, by W.H. Bartlett and engraved by J. Carter, 1840. This was one local hostelry that Burns did not patronize to any extent, but it still exists today as a public house and museum. 'Poosie Nansie' was the name that Burns bestowed upon the landlord's wife, Mrs Gibson. After dropping into this 'beggars' "ken" by chance late one evening and witnessing the revels of the 'randie gangrel bodies' assembled there, Burns used Poosie Nansie's as the setting for 'The Jolly Beggars':

> Ae night at e'en a merry core
> O' randie, gangrel bodies,
> In Poosie Nansie's held the splore,
> To drink their orra duddies:
> Wi' quaffing and laughing,
> They ranted an' they sang,
> Wi' jumping an' thumping,
> The vera girdle rang. . . .

Commenting on the piece which, although composed in 1785, did not see the light of day in print until after the poet's death, Thomas Carlyle wrote that 'the subject is truly among the lowest in Nature, but it only the more shows our Poet's gift in raising it into the domain of Art'.

The parish church, Mauchline, undated. A number of people associated with Burns are buried in the kirkyard, including the poet's friend and patron Gavin Hamilton, Nance Tannock, 'Poosie Nansie' and several of Burns's children who died in infancy. 'Racer Jess' is also buried here. She was the daughter of George Gibson and 'Poosie Nansie' and is referred to in 'The Holy Fair'.

The kirkyard at Mauchline, undated – the setting for Burns's satire 'The Holy Fair':

> Here stands a shed to fend the show'rs,
> An screen our countra gentry;
> There 'Racer Jess', an twa-three whores
> Are blinking at the entry.
> Here sits a raw o' tittlin' jads,
> Wi' heavin' breasts an' bare neck;
> An' there a batch o' wabster lads,
> Blackguardin frae Kilmarnock,
>   For fun this day.
>
> Here some are thinkin' on their sins,
> An' some upo' their claes;
> Ane curses feet that fyl'd his shins,
> Anither sighs an' prays:
> On this hand sits a chosen swatch,
> Wi' screwed-up, grace-proud faces;
> On that a set o' chaps, at watch,
> Thrang winkin' on the lasses
>   To chairs that day. . . .

Opposite: A scene from 'The Holy Fair', illustrated by J.M. Wright and engraved by J. Rogers, 1839. The piece was composed in the autumn of 1785 and is said to reflect fairly accurately (allowing for the use of poetic licence) the celebration of Holy Communion at Mauchline on the second Sunday of August in that year. 'It is no doubt', wrote the 'Ettrick Shepherd' James Hogg, 'a reckless piece of satire, but it is a clever one, and must have cut to the bone. But much as I admire the poem, 'he added, 'I must regret that it is partly borrowed from Fergusson['s 'Leith Races'].'

Ballochmyle House near Mauchline, early 1900s. Once owned by Sir John Whitefoord, with whom Burns was acquainted as a fellow Freemason, the estate is now occupied by Ballochmyle Hospital. Sir John was forced to part with the property in 1784 (it was bought by Claud Alexander) after the failure of the Ayr Bank some years earlier, and Burns acknowledged the change in his friend's circumstances by writing 'Farewell to Ballochmyle': 'Fareweel, the bonie banks of Ayr,/Fareweel, fareweel! sweet Ballochmyle!' Burns himself explained that he composed the verses 'on the amiable and excellent family of Whitefoords leaving Ballochmyle, when Sir John's misfortunes had obliged him to sell the estate'.

The Fog House on the Ballochmyle estate. This wooden summerhouse, erected by Claud Alexander in the grounds of his property, marks the spot where, in 1786, Burns saw Alexander's sister Wilhelmina walking by herself. She became the inspiration for 'The Lass o' Ballochmyle', which Burns composed during that year. 'I had roved out . . . in the favourite haunts of my Muse, on the banks of the Ayr' he explained 'when . . . I spied one of the fairest pieces of Nature's workmanship that ever crowned the poetic landscape, or met a poet's eye.' The Fog House burned down in 1944.

A scene from 'The Lass o' Ballochmyle', captured by J.M. Wright. This engraving by J. Rogers was published in 1839.

With careless step I onward stray'd,
My heart rejoic'd in nature's joy,
When, musing in a lonely glade,
A maiden fair I chanc'd to spy:
Her look was like the morning's eye,
Her air like nature's vernal smile;
Perfection whisper'd, passing by,
'Behold the lass o' Ballochmyle!'

Burns was living at Mossgiel when this famous portrait of him was painted by the Edinburgh-born artist Alexander Nasmyth in 1787. The poet was in his late twenties and basking in the success of the Kilmarnock edition of his *Poems, Chiefly in the Scottish Dialect*, which had been issued the previous year. Nasmyth's portrait was commissioned (although the artist undertook the work free of charge) to decorate the first Edinburgh edition of Burns's *Poems*. In 1828 Nasmyth painted a full-length portrait of the poet for use in Lockhart's biography.

A portrait of Jean Armour Burns (Mrs Robert Burns). The poet's wife, who lived from 1767 to 1834, was captured here during her later years in a watercolour executed by Samuel MacKenzie in about 1820. Writing to a friend, Burns described Jean, one of his 'Belles of Mauchline', as having 'the most placid good nature and sweetness of disposition; a warm heart . . . vigorous health and sprightly cheerfulness, set off to the best advantage by a more than commonly handsome figure'.

CHAPTER FOUR

AROUND ELLISLAND

Ellisland Farm, Dunscore, *c.* 1910. The property lies beside the River Nith about 6 miles north-west of Dumfries, and Burns leased it from Patrick Miller (who owned the Dalswinton estate) at an annual rental of £50 for the first three years, rising to £70 thereafter. The 170-acre farm was badly run down when Burns came into possession of it, so he was given £300 with which to build a farmhouse and to fence the fields. The house building proved to be such a long-winded affair that, although Burns had signed the lease for Ellisland in March 1788 (and began working on the farm in June), he did not actually move into the farmhouse with Jean and their children until the middle of the following year. However, despite Burns's best efforts the farm was not a success and, within six months of settling his family there, he took up a post as an Exciseman at a salary of £50 per annum to augment his income. By January 1790 he was telling his brother Gilbert that 'this farm has undone my enjoyment of myself. It is a ruinous affair on all hands. But let it go to hell!' He quit Ellisland in the autumn of 1791 and moved to Dumfries. The property was farmed until 1921, when it was purchased by a former President of the Edinburgh Burns Club and later given to the nation. The land is still used for grazing, but the restored farmhouse (with its collection of Burnsiana) may be visited, along with the nearby refurbished granary which was opened in 1979 as a museum of farming life.

Opposite: The 'Tam o' Shanter' Walk, Ellisland. The gate seen here leads to a wooded walk along the banks of the Nith, and it is said that Burns composed many famous lines while wandering in this much-loved spot. The plaque reads: 'One autumn day in 1790 Robert Burns paced up and down this grassy path crooning to himself in one of his poetical moods the words which became the immortal tale of "Tam o' Shanter". In the last field along the path the poet saw the wounded hare that inspired the "Address to the Wounded Hare".'

This early engraving of Ellisland Farm, portraying it as the rural idyll that it manifestly was not, appeared on a postcard bearing the legend 'Where Robert Burns – the national poet of Scotland – took up house with his newly-wedded wife, Jean Armour. In the stockyard at Ellisland Burns wrote the sublime poem "To Mary in Heaven", and while dannering along the path by the River Nith he composed the immortal "Tam o' Shanter".'

Dalswinton House north-west of Dumfries, 1930s (above), and the mirror-like surface of Dalswinton Loch (below). The mansion pictured here was built by Patrick Miller, who became acquainted with Burns while the poet was in Edinburgh during 1786 and offered him the tenancy of Ellisland, which comprised part of the Dalswinton estate at that time. A steamboat pioneered by Miller, and whose engine was built by William Symington, a mining engineer at Wanlockhead, was launched on Dalswinton Loch on 14 October 1788, since when a debate has simmered away concerning whether or not Burns was actually present for the occasion. Tradition asserts that Burns was one of the passengers aboard the vessel on that historic day, although there is considerable room for doubt. Burns himself seems never to have mentioned the incident in his work or correspondence, and he probably would have done so had he been an eye-witness. Yet, as James Mackay observes in his *Burns-Lore of Dumfries and Galloway* (1988), given that the poet was at Ellisland on the day in question, 'it seems plausible that [he] would have taken an hour from his harvesting . . . to see an event which must have been the talk of that quiet countryside'.

Friars' Carse on the banks of the River Nith, late 1940s. When Burns was the tenant farmer at neighbouring Ellisland, the mansion and estate were owned by Captain Robert Riddell with whom the poet quickly struck up a friendship. They parted on bad terms, however, some months before Riddell's death in April 1794, but Burns always retained fond memories of Friars' Carse and he paid tribute to the family, and particularly to the man who shared his keen interest in folk music. 'At their fireside,' he wrote, 'I have enjoyed more pleasant evenings than at all the houses of fashionable people in this country put together; and to their kindness and hospitality I am indebted for many of the happiest hours of my life.'

The Hermitage at Friars' Carse. This photograph was almost certainly taken by John Rutherford in 1896. (Rutherford, a man of many parts, was once the official photographer to Dumfries Prison.) The Hermitage, built in the grounds of his estate by Captain Riddell, was used as a small summerhouse. It lay close to the boundary with Ellisland (indeed it may still be seen) and, as a favoured neighbour and guest, Burns was allowed to use it. It was here in 1788 that he wrote the lines beginning 'Thou whom chance may hither lead/ Be thou clad in russet weed . . .' (from 'Verses in Friars' Carse Hermitage').

A leisurely scene captured outside the Auldgirth Inn, early 1900s (above), 2 miles or so north of Ellisland. This old inn dates back to the sixteenth century, and was conveniently placed in those days to provide overnight accommodation for the monks and pilgrims of Melrose Abbey when they travelled from the Borders to the coast of Galloway. This ancient connection is recalled by the cross which is just visible here in the main chimney-stack (and still a distinctive feature of the building today). Burns would have been familiar with the inn which, in his time, not only served as a hostelry but as the local smithy as well. Situated just off the busy A76 trunk road, the Auldgirth Inn continues to flourish, although a once-famous landmark known as the 'Three Brethren' (a tree with three trunks that Burns would have seen many times) was destroyed during the nineteenth century. Auldgirth Bridge (below) is pictured here in 1918. Built in 1782, the stone bridge has not carried road traffic since it was bypassed by the A76 some years ago, although it is still open to pedestrians. Burns would have crossed it often during his travels.

The King's Arms and Kirkgate, Dunscore, early 1900s (above) and Main Street, Dunscore, late nineteenth century (below). The village lies to the west of Ellisland, and it was here in 1789 that Burns and his friend Captain Robert Riddell of nearby Friars' Carse founded the library of the Monkland Friendly Society. The library society originally operated from Monkland Cottage but eventually moved to a house in Main Street. Writing in 1791, Burns explained the purpose of the enterprise: 'To store the minds of the lower classes with useful knowledge is certainly of very great consequence, both to them as individuals and to society at large,' he declared. 'Giving them a turn for reading and reflection is giving them a source of innocent and laudable amusement; and besides, raises them to a more dignified degree in the scale of rationality. . . . The plan [is] so simple', Burns continued, 'as to be practicable in any corner of the country; and so useful as to deserve the notice of every country gentleman who thinks the improvement of that part of his own species, whom chance has thrown into the humble walks of the peasant and the artisan, a matter worthy of his attention.'

The former Brownhill Inn, situated just south of Closeburn on what is nowadays the A76 trunk route between Dumfries and Kilmarnock. In the days of the stagecoach Brownhill was an important landmark, being the first changing place for horses coming north from Dumfries. The inn is pictured on the left of this photograph with the stables on the opposite side of the road. The Wordsworths and Coleridge spent a night at Brownhill while on their tour through Scotland in 1803, and Burns was a frequent recipient of its hospitality, particularly when out on his Excise duties. 'I fancied to myself while I was sitting in the parlour,' Dorothy Wordsworth confided to her journal, 'that Burns might have caroused there . . . and this thought gave a melancholy interest to the smoky walls. It was as pretty a room as a thoroughly dirty one could be – a square parlour painted green, but so covered over with smoke and dirt that it looked not unlike green seen through black gauze.' John Bacon was the landlord in the poet's day, and he crops up more than once in Burns's work. For example, he appears as the inspiration behind 'The Henpecked Husband':

> Curs'd be the man, the poorest wretch in life,
> The crouching vassal to a tyrant wife!
> Who has no will but by her high permission;
> Who has not sixpence but in her possession. . . .

However, he is more obviously the subject of the following clever epigram, composed on the spur of the moment while the poet was dining at the inn one evening:

> At Brownhill we always get dainty good cheer,
> And plenty of bacon each day in the year;
> We've a' thing that's nice, and mostly in season,
> But why always Bacon – come tell me the reason?

CHAPTER FIVE
DUMFRIES

Kelton, a hamlet by the River Nith a few miles south of Dumfries, *c.* 1910. The smuggling vessel *Rosamond* was repaired at a boatyard here, after it had been seized by Burns and his fellow Excisemen during an incident at Sarkfoot near Gretna in 1792.

The New (Buccleuch) Bridge, Dumfries, pictured here a few years before it was strengthened and improved in 1935. Completed in 1794 when Burns was living at Millbrae Vennel (now Burns Street), the New Bridge was designed by local architect Thomas Boyd, who had earlier supervised the building of the farmhouse at Ellisland. Formerly linking the neighbouring burghs of Dumfries and Maxwelltown before their amalgamation in 1929, the New Bridge was a great asset to the town when it opened. The leisurely scene above would be unimaginable today, although the weight of traffic crossing the river at this point has eased since the opening of the Dumfries bypass.

Two views of Bank Street, Dumfries. Above, looking towards Whitesands and the River Nith during the early 1900s, the house where Burns lived is seen on the right. Below, looking along Bank Street in the opposite direction towards High Street, *c.* 1920, the house is pictured on the left. Burns and his family moved to the town from Ellisland in November 1791, and occupied just three rooms on an upper floor of the property. The building stood in what was then officially called the Wee Vennel but which, for obvious reasons in that age of open sewers, had been dubbed locally the Stinking Vennel. (The house itself is still standing despite a chequered history, but it is privately owned and NOT open to the public.) The Bank Street flat must have seemed very small to Burns and his family after their more spacious quarters at Ellisland. The birth of another child in 1792 prompted the move to larger premises in Millbrae Vennel (later called Mill Street and now Burns Street) in May 1793. A plaque placed on the Bank Street property in 1971 records the dates of Burns's occupation in what is called the 'Songhouse of Scotland', where the bard is said to have completed over sixty poems and songs during his eighteen months' residence.

Dock Park looking towards St Michael's Bridge, Dumfries, *c.* 1938. Stretching along the east bank of the River Nith between Whitesands and Castledykes, this area of open ground was a favourite haunt of Burns and he frequently took a stroll here. More energetically, perhaps, on 26 March 1795 the poet assembled at Dock Park with his comrades for the first parade of the Royal Dumfries Volunteers. Apparently the one hundred or so men who comprised the RDV were not required to march more than 5 miles from the town, inspiring Burns to offer the following toast at a Volunteers' dinner: 'May we never see the French, nor the French see us.'

Looking south along the River Nith from the Old (Devorgilla's) Bridge, Dumfries, *c.* 1914. The building on the right perched almost at the water's edge close to the caul was once the town's eighteenth-century corn mill. It was used as such until 1911 and harnessed the Nith to power its grinding-wheel. Subsequently the building was turned into a hydro-electric station. In 1986, however, the premises were transformed into the Robert Burns Centre, housing a bookshop, café-gallery and audio-visual theatre (used as a cinema in the evenings), with displays and exhibitions telling the story of Burns's last years spent in the Dumfries of the 1790s.

The Old Bridge, Dumfries, spanning the River Nith and looking towards Whitesands with Buccleuch Street beyond, 1920s (above). The wintry scene pictured below, showing Maxwelltown and the Observatory, was captured in 1940 on one of those rare occasions when the river froze sufficiently hard for people to walk on the surface. The bridge is the oldest surviving multiple-arched stone bridge in Scotland, and owes its existence to the generosity of Lady Devorgilla, daughter of the first Lord of Galloway. The original structure was made of wood and replaced in the first half of the fifteenth century by the sandstone bridge of the present day. Floodlit at dusk, the six arches of the Old Bridge drenched in amber light are one of the town's most pleasing features. Of course, Burns was familiar with every inch of the Old Bridge and doubtless crossed it many times on his travels around Dumfries, particularly on those occasions when he elected to call for some refreshment at the hostelry which in the poet's day served the 'Brig End' of the town, and for many years occupied the premises now given over to the Old Bridge House Museum.

The River Nith from Burns Walk, Dumfries, 1920s. The banks of the Nith were a favourite haunt of the poet and, during the last few years of his life, he often wandered out of the town northwards to Lincluden or downstream to Castledykes, no doubt seeking inspiration as he went. The Nith is a long river, rising near Cumnock and pursuing a winding course for more than 70 miles before flowing into the Solway Firth. The river that was so much a part of Burns's life was mentioned in more than one of his poems and songs. Perhaps he waxed most lyrically on the subject in 'The Banks of Nith':

> How lovely, Nith, thy fruitful vales,
> Where bounding hawthorns gayly bloom;
> And sweetly spread thy sloping dales,
> Where lambkins wanton through the broom.
> Tho' wandering now must be my doom,
> Far from thy bonie banks and braes,
> May there my latest hours consume,
> Amang the friends of early days!

Burns Walk (on the northern edge of Dumfries) is well signposted today, allowing anyone with an interest in the poet literally to tread in his footsteps, although whether Burns himself would recognize the modern landscape is highly debatable.

Looking north along the River Nith from Kingholm towards Dumfries, early 1900s. 'I love thee Nith thy banks and braes', wrote Burns.

A lone cat weaves its way past the Old Bridge House, Dumfries, 1950s. Erected in 1660, the sandstone building was a simple dwelling house at first, although it later became an inn and continued as such until the end of the nineteenth century when it reverted to its original purpose. This was just one of the hostelries used by Burns during his years in Dumfries. Thought to be the town's oldest house, the building has now been converted into a museum of local everyday life, and includes the reconstruction of an 1850s' kitchen, an 1870s' bedroom, an early dentist's surgery and a Victorian nursery.

Queensberry Square and Great King Street, Dumfries, late 1930s. Nowadays the centre of the Square is dominated by the Queensberry Monument, designed by Robert Adam and erected in 1778. Its absence from this photograph is owing to the fact that the memorial was moved in 1935 and placed in front of the town's County Buildings (later the Regional Council Offices) in English Street. However, in 1990 the column was restored to its original site. On 4 June 1795 Burns, who was a founder member of the Royal Dumfries Volunteers (formed to help maintain law and order at home during the French Revolutionary Wars), paraded into the Square with his comrades when the Volunteers received their colours in the shadow of the Queensberry Monument before dining together at the King's Arms. In April 1795 (three months after the Volunteers' formation) Burns wrote 'Does Haughty Gaul Invasion Threat?' – sometimes called 'The Dumfries Volunteers' – which first appeared in the *Dumfries Journal* of 5 May that year. The rousing ballad was an instant success, effectively harnessing the patriotic mood of the country at that time, and it was immediately copied by other newspapers and periodicals including the *Caledonian Mercury* and the *Scots Magazine*:

> Does haughty Gaul invasion threat?
> Then let the louns beware, sir;
> There's wooden walls upon our seas,
> And Volunteers on shore Sir. . . .
>
> . . .
>
> O let us not, like snarling curs,
> In wrangling be divided,
> Till, slap! come in an unco loun,
> And wi' a rung decide it!
> Be Britain still to Britain true,
> Amang ourselves united;
> For never but by British hands
> Maun British wrangs be righted. . . .

An undated photograph showing the original bar of the County Hotel, Dumfries. Earlier known as the Commercial Hotel and situated in the town's High Street opposite the fountain, the building (used as a private residence in Burns's day) was demolished during the 1980s although its façade was retained. Bonnie Prince Charlie stayed at the hotel for a few days in late 1745 and – inevitably, perhaps – a room, appropriately carpeted in the Royal Stuart tartan, was named after him. There was also a Burns Room which contained the library of Miss Jean Armour Burns Brown, together with other items associated with her illustrious great-grandfather.

Part of St Michael's Street, Dumfries, early 1900s. After leaving the Midsteeple on 25 July 1796, Burns's funeral procession moved slowly along the High Street, Nith Place and finally St Michael's Street, before arriving at the church pictured here (centre). (Meanwhile, the poet's widow was giving birth to her ninth child nearby.) Burns was accorded a military send-off, with his bier being supported by members of the Royal Dumfries Volunteers. Dumfries had never witnessed a scene like it and, according to one estimate, 12,000 mourners lined the route while all the church bells of the town tolled at intervals.

The Globe, Dumfries, *c.* 1900. Burns pilgrims from all over the world are drawn to this early seventeenth-century hostelry tucked away in a close just off the town's High Street. The Globe was famously described by Burns as his 'favourite howff' and he was a frequent visitor to it, not only when residing in Dumfries but also while living at Ellisland. There are many items on display here relating to the poet and a Burns Room downstairs contains his chair and a collection of Burnsiana. Mrs Smith was the landlady at the time this photograph was taken, and she remained in post until the 1920s. Globe Inn Close itself was the subject of a restoration project during the Burns bicentenary year of 1996. Among various new installations marking Burns's connection with the Globe and its precincts are several iron sculptures depicting scenes from 'Tam o' Shanter', and a block of Locharbriggs red sandstone on which have been inscribed the opening lines from 'Ae Fond Kiss'. The poet himself is said to have scratched the following lines from 'At the Globe Tavern, Dumfries' on a window-pane there:

> I murder hate by field or flood,
> Tho' Glory's name may screen us;
> In wars at hame I'll spend my blood –
> Life-giving wars of Venus.
> The deities that I adore
> Are Social Peace and Plenty:
> I'm better pleas'd to make one more,
> Than be the death of twenty.

The Globe and Globe Inn Close seen from the opposite direction, late nineteenth century. The Globe is probably one of the oldest hostelries in Scotland (it was established in 1610) and remains an extremely popular watering-hole today. However, you could be forgiven for thinking that barely a window-pane in the building has escaped the attention of Burns's diamond stylus at one time or another. Stanzas from 'Lovely Polly Stewart', 'Comin' Thro' the Rye', 'At the Globe Tavern, Dumfries' and 'Lines Written on Windows of the Globe Tavern' have all been inscribed there.

An undated photograph of the Observatory at the top of Corberry Hill, Dumfries. Originally housing a stone windmill, the tower was established as an astronomical observatory and museum in 1835. The museum complex now boasts collections drawn from throughout Dumfries and Galloway and the Camera Obscura, installed in 1836 and thought to be the oldest of its type still in use anywhere in the world, serves as a major tourist attraction.

Below: An interior view of the Dumfries Burgh Museum. Note the spiral staircase which has been constructed around a ship's mast. The timber was originally pressed into service as a centre post in the days when the building was still used as a windmill, and it was reputedly taken from a smuggling vessel captured in the Solway during Burns's time as an Exciseman.

The King's Arms, English Street, Dumfries, *c.* 1950. No longer in existence (Boots the Chemist now occupies the site), this was one of the town's oldest hotels. Burns scratched these lines on one of its window-panes:

> Ye men of wit and wealth, why all this sneering
> 'Gainst poor Excisemen? Give the cause a hearing:
> What are your Landlord's rent-rolls? – taxing ledgers!
> What Premiers? – what ev'n Monarchs? – mighty Gaugers!
> Nay, what are Priests? (those seeming godly wise-men),
> What are they, pray, but Spiritual Excisemen!

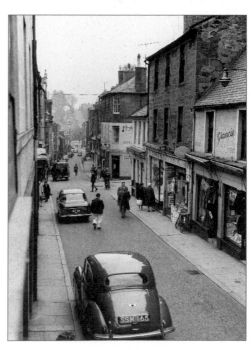

Looking down Friars' Vennel from Church Place to the River Nith, Dumfries, 1961. Burns could have passed along this narrow and congested aperture many times in the days when it served as the main link between the High Street and the New Bridge. Burns's epigram:

> Lord to account who dares thee call,
> Or e'er dispute Thy pleasure?
> Else why within so thick a wall
> Enclose so poor a treasure?

was aimed at one of his political adversaries, Thomas Goldie, a local dignitary whose estate was Craigmuie near Moniaive but who, when in town, occupied a house near the foot of Friars' Vennel.

The Wide Entry, Dumfries, looking towards the High Street from Loreburn Street, 1890s. The Wide Entry was demolished during the 1920s to make way for Great King Street. Queensberry Square, which was laid out in 1770 and where Burns later paraded with the Royal Dumfries Volunteers, is located beyond the arch pictured at the far end of the Wide Entry.

The substantial house in what is now called Burns Street, Dumfries, where the poet ended his days. He lived here from May 1793 until his death on 21 July 1796. By the time this photograph was taken in the early 1900s the original red sandstone from which the building was constructed had been plastered over, thereby considerably detracting from the external appearance of the place.

Workmen chipping away at the exterior of Burns House to reveal the original stonework beneath, 1934. This formed part of an extensive restoration programme during which the property was returned more or less to the condition it was in when the poet lived there. The house now serves as a museum, and it has become a vital place of pilgrimage for Burns devotees from around the globe.

St. Michael's Church, Dumfries, early 1920s. Burns's funeral service was conducted here and his remains interred in the north-east corner of the churchyard. Burns and his family attended worship at St Michael's during their years in Dumfries and, although their box-pew has long since disappeared, a brass plate shows its position. In 1989 windows honouring the poet and his wife were installed to mark the centenary of the Dumfries Burns Howff Club, whose members also organised a project to erect a plaque in the churchyard, denoting the various locations of more than forty friends and contemporaries of the poet who were also buried there.

Below: Lincluden Abbey, Dumfries, 1950s. The remains of this twelfth-century convent for Benedictine nuns (later it became a college with twelve bedesmen and a provost) were a favourite haunt of Burns during his riverside rambles north of the town, and he immortalized them in a song:

As I stood by yon roofless tower,
Where the wa'flow'r scents the dewy air,
Where the houlet mourns in her ivy bower,
And tells the midnight moon her care. . . .

Shakespeare Street, Dumfries, *c.* 1910. The lofty roof of Scotland's oldest working theatre, the Theatre Royal, can be glimpsed on the right. The theatre was opened on 29 September 1792 and Burns proved to be an enthusiastic patron. During the nineteenth century this 'pocket-edition of a theatre', as J.M. Barrie described it, 'where the audience in the dress circle . . . could almost shake hands with the man in the pit', attracted some of Britain's finest players, including Edmund Kean. Another great tragedian, William Charles Macready, appeared at the Theatre Royal during his earliest days on the stage, when his father leased the premises for four years from 1813.

Two views of Whitesands (or 'the Sands'), Dumfries, dating from the late nineteenth century (above) and *c*. 1910 (below). One of the former weekly livestock markets (when the waterfront pubs always enjoyed a brisk day's trading) can be seen in full swing in the bottom photograph, occupying the broad and nowadays busy artery that runs alongside the Nith. Because of its proximity to the river, Whitesands is prone to flooding, and sandbags are a depressingly familiar feature stacked outside the doorways of those premises whose basements are routinely invaded by water following periods of prolonged heavy rain. The Coach and Horses is one of the hostelries to be found on Whitesands and, although in Burns's day a question mark hung over the reputation of the house, no doubt the poet was persuaded to overlook that small matter in favour of its convenient position at the foot of Bank Street (the Wee or Stinking Vennel), a few short steps from his own front door.

The Midsteeple, Dumfries, 1950s. Completed in 1707 and restored in 1909, the Midsteeple has served over the years as a municipal building, courthouse and prison. Traditionally its precincts have always been a rallying point for the town; a place of ceremony and festival. During the eighteenth century the cattle drovers of Galloway gathered here when taking their beasts on the long journey south to market. Following his death Burns's body was removed from his house and placed in the courtroom of the Midsteeple, where it lay until his funeral. A year earlier, in 1795, the poet had mentioned the building in his patriotic ballad 'Does Haughty Gaul Invasion Threat?'.

An undated view of Terregles House, a few miles north-west of Dumfries. The property has since been demolished. The house was rebuilt in the eighteenth century by Lady Winifred Maxwell Constable, and Burns composed 'Nithsdale's Welcome Hame' to celebrate her return to the ancient family seat.

> The noble Maxwells and their powers
> Are coming o'er the border,
> And they'll gae big Terreagles' towers,
> And set them a' in order.
> And they declare Terreagles fair,
> For their abode they choose it;
> There's no a heart in a' the land
> But's lighter at the news o't. . . .

The gardens at Terregles, 1890s.

CHAPTER SIX
A BURNS-EYE VIEW (1): LANDSCAPE, TOWNS & VILLAGES

A panoramic view (undated) of New Abbey, with Criffel behind and the ruins of Sweetheart Abbey in the foreground. The village developed in the thirteenth century beside its Cistercian abbey, the building of which is recalled in a stone carving set in the wall of a local cottage, and believed to celebrate the efforts of three women who ferried red sandstone across the nearby Solway Firth.

> The Nith shall run to Corsicon
> And Criffel sink in Solway,
> Ere we permit a Foreign Foe
> On British ground to rally!

wrote Burns in 1795, when rumours of a French invasion were rife.

A solitary vehicle meanders through the lonely Dalveen Pass, 1950s. This is a remote stretch of road that winds through the Lowther Hills on its way from Durisdeer to Elvanfoot. Burns referred to it as 'the lang glen' (the name by which it is known locally) in the opening line of 'The Braw Wooer', one of the poet's later works and described by a contemporary as 'a pearl of great price' among his songs.

The Roaring Linn, Glen Afton

Afton Water, which flows through Glen Afton to New Cumnock, 1930s. Referring to his song 'Sweet Afton', Burns himself described Afton Water as possessing 'some charming, wild scenery on its banks. I have a particular pleasure in those little pieces of poetry such as our Scots songs etc. where the names and landskip-features of rivers, lakes or woodlands that one knows are introduced. I attempted a compliment of this kind to Afton. . . .'

The road through Glen Afton, *c.* 1910.

Flow gently, sweet Afton! among thy green braes,
Flow gently, I'll sing thee a song in thy praise;
My Mary's asleep by the murmuring stream,
Flow gently, sweet Afton, disturb not her dream.

· · ·

How pleasant thy banks and green valleys below,
Where, wild in the woodlands, the primroses blow;
There oft, as mild Ev'ning weeps over the lea,
The sweet-scented birk shades my Mary and me. . . .

The Mennock Pass, coursing through the Lowther Hills, 1920s. Dorothy Wordsworth (travelling with her brother William and Samuel Taylor Coleridge) recorded her impressions of the pass in 1803, after visiting Burns's grave in Dumfries and later glimpsing Ellisland en route. The party left Thornhill and 'turned up a hill to the right, the road for a little way was very steep, bare hills with sheep. . . . The simplicity of the prospect impressed us very much; we now felt indeed that we were in Scotland. . . . There was no room in the vale but for the river and the road; we had sometimes the stream to the right, sometimes to the left. . . .'

Mines at Leadhills, *c.* 1920. Although just over the old county boundary in Lanarkshire, Burns would have been familiar with this village situated only a mile or two from Wanlockhead and the birthplace, incidentally, of another (although less renowned) Scottish poet, Allan Ramsay, whose father managed Lord Hopetoun's mines here. 'The trees told of the coldness of the climate,' wrote Dorothy Wordsworth, '[and] here, as at Wanlockhead, were haycocks, hay-stacks, potato-beds and kail-garths in every possible variety of shape. . . . Indeed, I should think that a painter might make several beautiful pictures in this village.'

The Solway shore near Annan, 1950s. This stretch of water, with the Cumbrian fells providing a magnificent backdrop on the English side, was deeply familiar to Burns during his days as an Exciseman and also in the last sad weeks of his life. Note the line of trees bent over in the direction of the prevailing wind, giving some indication of the mighty south-westerly gales that sweep in from the Irish Sea across this exposed part of the country.

Penpont near Thornhill, *c.* 1905. James A. Mackay, writing in his *Burns-Lore of Dumfries and Galloway* (1988), records that during Burns's time the parish of Penpont boasted less than 1,000 inhabitants of whom barely a tenth resided in the village itself. Nevertheless, the community was served by seven pubs, and it was outside one of these establishments that Burns was set upon by smugglers in the course of his Excise duties.

The Devil's Beef Tub, 1920s. Situated along the winding route between Moffat and the Crook Inn at Tweedsmuir, Burns would have been well acquainted with this yawning depression in the hills – over 600 ft deep and half a mile across at the top – in the course of his travels. Employing this hollow for a scene in his novel *Redgauntlet*, Scott described it as 'a deep, black, blackguardly-looking abyss of a hole . . . [which] goes straight down from the roadside as perpendicularly as it can go'. Nowadays this exposed spot is one of Upper Annandale's great tourist attractions.

This 1930s' tourist postcard view of Moffatdale records the unchanging contours of the hills in a scene that would have been instantly familiar to Burns a century and a half earlier.

The Grey Mare's Tail, 1930s. South-west Scotland boasts at least three waterfalls of this name: one near Thornhill, another in the Galloway Forest Park and that which is pictured here. Lying 10 miles north-east of Moffat on the road to Selkirk, this is by far the most impressive of the trio, with its 300 ft drop set against spectacular mountain scenery. Local opinion differs about how the waterfall acquired its name, although one favourite theory suggests that it might be a reference to the incident in 'Tam o' Shanter' when Tam's grey mare 'left behind her ain grey tail' while being pursued across a bridge over the Doon.

Carsethorn, *c.* 1925. Situated on the coast at the point where the River Nith flows into the Solway Firth, the village was a thriving outport serving Dumfries during the eighteenth century; a place from where many people emigrated to the 'New World', and where vessels too large to navigate the Nith were able to unload their cargoes. As such, Carsethorn was well known to Burns the Exciseman. The village, resting below the towering hump of Criffel in an area dubbed 'the garden of Galloway', is now a popular holiday resort, enjoying magnificent views over the Solway to the Cumbrian fells beyond.

Ecclefechan, 1920s. Lying in the shadow of Burnswark, the village is famous for being Thomas Carlyle's birthplace. The historian and essayist was born here in 1795, the year before Burns's death. Ecclefechan enjoyed some degree of prosperity in those days when weaving was the inhabitants' main occupation. Burns visited the place a few times in his capacity as an Exciseman and, in February 1795, the poet was marooned there in a heavy snowstorm. 'To add to my misfortune,' he wrote to a friend, 'since dinner a scraper has been torturing catgut in sounds that would have insulted the dying agonies of a sow under the hands of a butcher. . . .'

Sark Bridge, early 1900s. Forming part of the boundary between England and Scotland, the River Sark flows into the Solway Firth just below Gretna. As an Exciseman, Burns took part in the capture of the *Rosamond* at Sarkfoot in 1792, although accounts of his involvement vary. As a poet, he mentions the river in the lines:

> Now Sark rins over Solway sands,
> An' Tweed rins to the ocean,
> To mark where England's province stands –
> Such a parcel of rogues in a nation!

Looking north along Lochmaben's broad High Street, late 1920s. Nestling in mid-Annandale, Lochmaben is one of the oldest Royal Burghs in Scotland, having been granted that status in 1447. Burns occasionally stayed at the manse here as a guest of the Revd Andrew Jaffray, when passing through the district on Excise business. Alluding to the fact that Lochmaben is set among a number of lochs, Burns referred to it as 'Marjory o' the mony Lochs/A Carlin auld and teugh . . . ' in one of his election ballads, 'The Five Carlins'. Half a century after the poet's death a Parliamentary Gazetteer described the place as 'dingy, desolate and leaden-eyed'.

High Street, Sanquhar, 1950s. Burns often stopped at this Upper Nithsdale town when travelling between Ellisland and Mauchline. Almost invariably he stayed at the New Arms in the High Street, later called the Queensberry Arms but no longer in existence. According to Burns it was 'the only tolerable inn in the place'. The inn was kept in the poet's day by Edward Whigham and a plaque, erected on the site in 1996 to mark the bicentenary of Burns's death, records the lines once inscribed by Burns on a window-pane there:

> Envy, if thy jaundiced eye
> Through this window chance to pry,
> To thy sorrow thou shalt find
> All that's generous, all that's kind,
> Friendship, virtue, every grace,
> Dwelling in this happy place.

Burns happened to be staying at Whigham's one night in January 1789 when the funeral cortège bearing Mrs Oswald of Auchencruive arrived at the inn. Burns hadn't known the lady personally, but he knew by local reputation that she was disliked by her tenants and servants. 'The frost was keen, and the grim evening and howling wind were ushering in a night of snow and drift,' the poet complained. 'My horse and I were both fatigued . . . and just as my friend and I were bidding defiance to the storm over a smoking bowl, in whirls the funeral pageantry of the late great Mrs Oswald, and poor I am forced to brave all the horrors of the tempestuous night, and jade my horse twelve miles further on, through the wildest moors and hills of Ayrshire to New Cumnock, the next inn,' Here, Burns sat down and composed his 'Ode, Sacred to the Memory of Mrs Oswald of Auchencruive'.

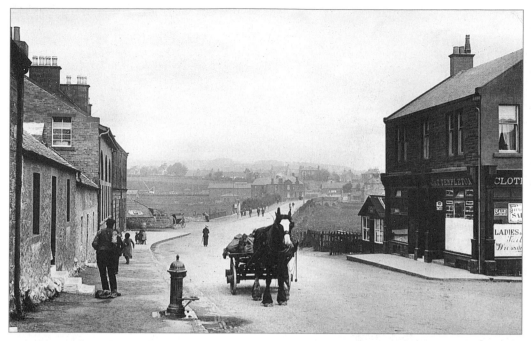

New Cumnock, *c.* 1915, where in January 1789 Burns wrote his 'Ode, Sacred to the Memory of Mrs Oswald. . .'. 'The powers of poesy and prose sunk under me when I would describe what I felt,' Burns wrote to a friend after arriving from Sanquhar. 'Suffice it to say, that when a good fire at New Cumnock had so far recovered my frozen sinews, I sat down and wrote the enclosed Ode.'

Southerness Lighthouse on the Solway, pictured here in the 1950s, boasts a connection with that same Mrs Oswald who – albeit posthumously – so rudely interrupted Burns's convivial evening at Sanquhar. For it was she who arranged that the lighthouse should be heightened in the late eighteenth century.

Wanlockhead, pictured above during the early 1920s, is Scotland's highest village. The photograph below shows what, in August 1909, was claimed to be Scotland's highest inhabited house. The village has no shortage of literary connections. The novelist Tobias Smollett, for example, who was related by marriage to one of the partners in a local mining company, reputedly wrote at least part of *Humphry Clinker* while staying there in 1770. Dorothy Wordsworth, passing through in 1803, described it in her journal as 'a wild and singular spot'. In conjunction with neighbouring Leadhills, home-grown literary talent includes the poets Robert Reid and Allan Ramsay. The former mining village (once called 'God's treasure-house in Scotland') whose mines, together with those at Leadhills, accounted for about 80 per cent of all Scottish lead at the height of their output, is surrounded by the Lowther Hills and was visited by Burns on his travels. Arriving there one winter's day in 1789–90, and unable to get his horse's shoes adapted for the icy conditions, he was prompted to compose some lines on the subject. 'Pegasus at Wanlockhead' (the poet's horse was called Pegasus) concludes:

> Ye Vulcan's sons of Wanlockhead,
> Pity my sad disaster;
> My Pegasus is poorly shod,
> I'll pay you like my master.

The road to Moffat Well, *c*. 1909 (above) and the building housing Moffat Well, *c*. 1900 (below). Dominated by the sandstone peak of Hart Fell and tucked into a fold of the Southern Uplands, Moffat was transformed from a rather poor village consisting mainly of but-and-ben (or thatched single-storey) cottages into a popular spa resort after a sulphurous well was discovered in 1633 on what are now the northern outskirts of the town. By the late eighteenth century when Burns would have been a familiar figure in the area Moffat had firmly established itself as a favourite watering-place, filled with visitors throughout the season who came to sample the liquid that was memorably described by a nineteenth-century guidebook as 'resembling bilge water or the scourings of a foul gun'. The small building pictured below eventually fell into disrepair, but it was restored during the 1980s as a reminder of those far-off days when Moffat could claim to be 'the Cheltenham of Scotland'.

Brow Well (pictured in the left foreground) by the Solway, a few miles west of Annan, *c.* 1907. Burns spent several weeks here at the tail-end of his life, 'taking the waters' and bathing in the Solway on the recommendation of his doctor, in what proved to be a wholly unsuccessful (and probably ill-advised) attempt to recover his rapidly failing health. Hundreds of people attended the Brow Well Bicentenary Commemorative Service that was held here on 17 July 1996.

Clarencefield, *c.* 1905. The village lies about a mile north of Brow Well, and it was the place where Burns reputedly proffered his seal in lieu of cash to the local innkeeper as payment for a bottle of port (which the poet was recommended to drink for medicinal purposes). 'I have been a week at sea-bathing,' Burns informed his brother Gilbert from the hamlet of Brow in early July 1796, 'and I will continue there or in a friend's house in the country all the summer. God help my wife and children if I am taken from their head! They will be poor indeed.' The poet returned to Dumfries on 18 July and died three days later.

Ruthwell, 1920s. The village lies barely a mile east of Brow Well and possesses several claims to fame. It houses what is arguably Scotland's finest Dark Age monument in the form of the seventh- or eighth century Ruthwell Cross. Furthermore, its minister for almost half a century from 1799 to 1843 was the Revd Henry Duncan, a man who, among other accomplishments, founded the Savings Bank movement at Ruthwell in 1810. As a young man Duncan had been introduced to Burns, and later he took an active part in the proceedings when plans were afoot to create the Burns Mausoleum in Dumfries.

The harbour at Girvan, c. 1915. Burns is said to have visited the Ship Inn at this small coastal town south of Ayr and legend has it that Nannie Brown, the publican's daughter, was the subject of Burns's song 'My Nanie O', which he composed when in his early twenties. 'Whether [the song] will stand the test I will not pretend to say, because it is my own. Only I can say it was, at the time, real,' he wrote somewhat enigmatically. Nannie Brown, it should be emphasized, was not the only contender for the song's heroine.

The Waterworks bridge on the Lochenbreck road near Gatehouse-of-Fleet, *c.* 1912. The caption on this postcard photograph declares that 'it was on coming over this old road that Burns wrote "Scots Wha Hae" (or "Robert Bruce's March to Bannockburn")'. John Syme, who accompanied Burns on a tour of Galloway in 1793 recounts how 'Scots Wha Hae' was composed during a storm of thunder, lightning and rain among the wilds of Glen Ken. In fact it was written, we are told, in the Murray Arms Hotel at Gatehouse when the pair stayed the night there.

A panoramic view of Galston east of Kilmarnock, with Loudoun Castle pictured in the distance, *c.* 1910. Together with neighbouring Newmilns and Darvel, Galston became renowned for lace-making after Huguenot and Dutch immigrants arrived in the seventeenth century.

> The rising sun owre Galston muirs
> Wi' glorious light was glintin;
> The hares were hirplin down the furrs,
> The lav'rocks they were chantin. . . .
> ('The Holy Fair')

Looking east along High Street, Annan, early 1900s, with the spire of Annan Old Parish Church rising in the distance. Burns usually lodged in the High Street when Excise duties called him to and around the town. He is thought to have composed 'The Deil's awa' wi' th' Exciseman' during an overnight stay at the place he referred to elsewhere as 'blinkin' Bess of Annandale,/That dwelt near Solway-side . . . .'.

The Cross, Kilmarnock, mid-1950s. In Burns's day the town's population was under 3,000 and the Cross was at the heart of the community. Nearby could be found Star Inn Close (since demolished) where, in July 1786, the first (or Kilmarnock) edition of Burns's *Poems, Chiefly in the Scottish Dialect* rolled off John Wilson's printing press. 'I threw off six hundred copies, of which I had got subscriptions for about two hundred and fifty,' Burns declared. 'My vanity was highly gratified by the reception I met with from the Publick; besides pocketing, all expenses deducted, near twenty pounds.'

Looking west along High Street, Kirkcudbright, *c.* 1903. E.A. Hornel, one of the group of Scottish artists known as the 'Glasgow Boys', lived here at Broughton House from 1901 until his death in 1933. The property, now in the care of the National Trust for Scotland, is open to the public and houses the painter's impressive library which includes the Kilmarnock, Edinburgh and Dublin editions of Burns's *Poems*. Excise duties brought Burns to Kirkcudbright (he also visited the town during his Galloway tour of 1793) when he stayed at the Heid Inn (now the Selkirk Arms) in the High Street.

Eglinton Street, Irvine, early 1900s. The town's Burns Club has amassed a fine collection of Burnsiana here in a house called Wellwood.

Drumlanrig Street, Thornhill, early 1900s (above) and West and East Morton Street, Thornhill, late 1950s (below). 'Passed through the village of Thornhill, built by the Duke of Queensberry,' recorded Dorothy Wordsworth in 1803. 'The "brother-houses" so small that they might have been built to stamp a character of insolent pride on his own huge mansion at Drumlanrigg [sic], which is in full view on the opposite side of the Nith.' James A. Mackay, writing in his *Burns-Lore of Dumfries and Galloway* (1988), quotes from an account given in the first half of the nineteenth century by a Professor Gillespie of St Andrew's who, as a young boy, witnessed an incident which throws an interesting light on the manner in which Burns conducted his Excise duties at Thornhill on one occasion. Suspecting that a poor innkeeper was harbouring contraband Burns asked her 'Kate, are ye mad? Dinna you know that the supervisor and I will be in upon you in the course of forty minutes?' Overhearing the exchange, Professor Gillespie declared that he 'had access to know that the friendly hint was not neglected'.

Ochiltree from the Cross, 1890s (above) and the Mill-Holm, Ochiltree, 1920s (below). Burns was acquainted with this hillside village lying west of Auchinleck, where the novelist George Douglas Brown was born in 1869. (Ochiltree appears as 'Barbie' in *The House with the Green Shutters*.) The subject of Burns's 'Epistle to James Tennant' was at one time the miller at Ochiltree Mill, and the village is mentioned in the poet's 'Epistle to William Simson':

> Ev'n winter bleak has charms to me,
> When winds rave thro' the naked tree;
> Or frosts on hills of Ochiltree
>   Are hoary gray;
> Or blinding drifts wild-furious flee
>   Dark'ning the day!

CHAPTER SEVEN

A BURNS-EYE VIEW (2): CASTLES & HOUSES (PUBLIC & PRIVATE)

Culzean Castle. Overlooking the Firth of Clyde, this mock-Gothic extravaganza was built by Robert Adam for the 10th Earl of Cassillis in 1777. Said to be one of the finest examples of an Adam house in Scotland, the property is now owned by the National Trust and – as such – it is open to the public. Burns referred to Culzean as 'Colean' in his poem 'Hallowe'en': 'Or for Colean the rout is ta'en,/ Beneath the moon's pale beams. . . .'

The Keep at Loudoun Castle near Galston, c. 1904. Following the death in 1786 of the 5th Earl of Loudoun, whose seat this was, Burns wrote 'Raving Winds around Her Blowing'. 'I composed these verses', the poet explained, 'on Miss Isabella Macleod of Rasa, alluding to her feelings on the death of her sister, and the still more melancholy death of her sister's husband, the late Earl of Loudoun, who shot himself out of sheer heart-break at some mortifications he suffered owing to the deranged state of his finances.'

An undated photograph of Closeburn Castle south-east of Thornhill. Burns became friendly with William Stewart who was the estate's factor, and of whom the following lines were composed:

> You're welcome, Willie Stewart,
> You're welcome, Willie Stewart,
> There's ne'er a flower that blooms in May,
> That's half sae welcome's thou art!

Drumlanrig Castle, Thornhill, late 1950s. 'This mansion', observed Dorothy Wordsworth in 1803, 'is indeed very large, but to us it appeared like a gathering together of little things. The roof is broken into a hundred pieces, cupolas etc., in the shape of casters, conjuror's balls, cups and the like. . . .' In Burns's day Drumlanrig was occupied by William the 4th Duke of Queensberry, of whom the poet famously wrote:

> All hail, Drumlanrig's haughty Grace –
> Discarded remnant of a race
> Once godlike. . . .

Caerlaverock Castle, south-east of Dumfries, *c.* 1907. Standing close to the Solway shore and the mouth of the River Nith, this ancient stronghold of the Maxwells (who first built a castle at Caerlaverock in the early thirteenth century) would have been a familiar landmark for Burns when travelling in the area on Excise duties.

Bonshaw Tower, south-east of Ecclefechan, *c.* 1934. Burns mentions Bonshaw in the third stanza of his song 'The Trogger':

> Then up we raise, and took the road
> And in by Ecclefechan,
> We brandy-stoup we gart it clink,
> And the strang-beer ream the quech in.
> Bedown the bents o' Bonshaw braes,
> We took the partin yokin. . . .

Hallheaths, Lochmaben, early 1900s. Built in 1866 but incorporating an earlier building dating from the 1770s, Hallheaths fell into disrepair and was demolished in the late 1940s, after it was vacated by the army who had occupied the premises during the Second World War. At one time there were a dozen farms on the estate, but nowadays it has become a pleasant spot for caravanning and camping holiday-makers. In 1795 the mansion was temporarily occupied by Burns's friend Maria Riddell, whom the poet described in one of his letters to her as 'thou first of Friends, and most accomplished of Women; even with all thy little caprices'.

Craigdarroch House, Moniaive, seen here in an undated photograph, was the home of 'Bonnie Annie Laurie' after her marriage to Alexander Fergusson. In Burns's day the couple's eldest son, also called Alexander, lived here. Not known as a cautious drinker, he was immortalized in 'The Whistle', a poem in which Burns describes a drinking contest held at Friars' Carse in 1789 on which occasion, so the story goes, Fergusson consumed sufficiently prodigious quantities of claret to win the event outright.

Auchamore Farm, Dunoon, *c.* 1905, where 'Highland Mary' (Mary Campbell) was born in 1763. A nursemaid in Gavin Hamilton's house at Mauchline during her early teens, Mary's relationship with Burns has been the subject of much scholarly speculation. The poet himself wrote:

> She has my heart, she has my hand,
> By secret troth and honor's band!
> 'Till the mortal stroke shall lay me low,
> I'm thine, my Highland lassie, O.

Laigh Park, 1920s. In addition to working Shanter Farm at Maidens west of Kirkoswald, Douglas Graham (the eponymous 'Tam o' Shanter' of Burns's poem) also farmed this nearby property.

An undated postcard view of Kirkconnell House, set between New Abbey and the west bank of the River Nith. The estate of Kirkconnell has been held by the Maxwells and their descendants since the early fifteenth century. The present mansion was built in the mid-eighteenth century by James Maxwell, whose son William was not only one of Burns's closest friends, but as a general practitioner working in Dumfries he was also the poet's medical adviser.

Netherplace House, Mauchline, c. 1919. The house was demolished during the 1940s, but it once belonged to a gentleman called William Campbell who died in 1786 and was reputed to have been much under his wife's thumb. Burns celebrated this unfortunate fact by making Campbell the subject of three different poems, of which this 'Epitaph on a Henpecked Squire' is a fair example:

> As father Adam first was fool'd
> (A case that's still too common),
> Here lies a man a woman ruled –
> The devil ruled the woman.

An undated photograph of a house built in 1840 and once known as Burns Cottage. It lies a few miles east of Moffat on the road to Selkirk and, standing on the banks of Moffat Water, the house has long been renamed Waterside. The building seen here occupies the site of an earlier wayside alehouse known as 'Willie's Mill' (not to be confused with the Tarbolton property of the same name), and reputed to be the spot where in the autumn of 1789 Burns met two of his Edinburgh friends, Alan Masterton and Willie Nicol. A convivial time was had by all, and the meeting was immortalized by Burns in his ballad 'Willie Brew'd a Peck o' Maut'. 'The occasion of it was this,' the poet explained. 'Mr William Nicol of the High School, Edinburgh, during the autumn being at Moffat, honest Allan (who was at that time on a visit to Dalswinton) and I went to pay Nicol a visit. We had such a joyous meeting that Mr Masterton and I agreed, each in his own way, that we should celebrate the business. . . . The air is Masterton's,' Burns added, 'the song mine.'

> O Willie brew'd a peck o' maut,
> And Rob and Allan cam to pree;
> Three blyther hearts, that lee-lang night,
> Ye wad na found in Christendie.
>
> . . .
>
> Here are we met, three merry boys,
> Three merry boys I trow are we;
> And mony a night we've merry been,
> And mony mae we hope to be! . . .

Craigieburn House, nestling in Craigieburn Wood below Hunterheck Hill east of Moffat. Craigieburn Wood was one of Burns's favourite haunts, and the poet told how his song of that name 'was composed on a passion which a Mr Gillespie, a particular friend of mine, had for a Miss Lorimer, afterwards a Mrs Whelpdale. The young lady was born in Craigieburn Wood.' Jean Lorimer was the 'Chloris' celebrated in some of Burns's later songs. Born in 1775, she was only about sixteen when the first version of 'Craigieburn Wood' was written. The verses given below form the second version of the song, composed in late 1794. 'The Lady on whom it was made,' commented Burns, 'is one of the finest women in Scotland; and, in fact . . . is in a manner to me what Sterne's Eliza was to him: a Mistress or Friend, or what you will, in the guileless simplicity of Platonic love.'

> Sweet fa's the eve on Craigieburn,
> And blythe awakes the morrow;
> But a' the pride o' Spring's return
> Can yield me nocht but sorrow.
>
> I see the flowers and spreading trees,
> I hear the wild birds singing;
> But what a weary wight can please,
> And Care his bosom wringing!
>
> Fain, fain would I my griefs impart,
> Yet dare na for your anger;
> But secret love will break my heart,
> If I conceal it langer.
>
> If thou refuse to pity me,
> If thou shalt love another,
> When yon green leaves fade frae the tree,
> Around my grave they'll wither.

St Mary's Isle, Kirkcudbright, *c.* 1900, where Burns spent an evening during his Galloway tour of 1793. John Syme, the poet's travelling companion, described the occasion. 'We got there about eight, just as they were at tea and coffee. . . . It is one of the most delightful places. We found some strangers at the Isle, and who else but Urbani [an Italian musician and composer]. Urbani sang us some Scotch songs accompanied with music. . . . We really had a treat of mental and sensual delight,' continued Syme, 'the latter consisting of delicious fruits etc. and the former you may conceive from the society, a company of 15 or 16 very agreeable young people.'

Dunlop House, Dunlop, *c.* 1903. This imposing building was the home of Mrs Frances Dunlop who, although many years older than Burns, was one of the poet's truest friends; a voluminous correspondence developed between them. They met originally after Mrs Dunlop had been introduced to Burns's work in 1786.

Dumcrieff, Moffat, lying on the banks of Moffat Water. Undoubtedly the most famous person to inhabit this property was John Loudon Macadam, the Ayr-born inventor and engineer whose name is forever linked with the 'macadamized' system of road-making. Shortly after Macadam quit the place Dumcrieff was purchased in 1792 by Dr James Currie, who became Burns's first (and later much criticized) editor and major biographer.

Catrine House, Catrine, where in October 1786 Burns dined with Lord Daer.

This wot ye all whom it concerns,
I Rhymer Robin alias Burns,
  October twenty-third,
A ne'er-to-be-forgotten day,
Sae far I sprackl'd up the brae,
  I dinner'd wi' a Lord.

Barskimming House, Mauchline, *c.* 1905. The estate – seat of Lord Barskimming, Lord Chief Justice of the Court of Session – was well-known territory for Burns.

> Thro' many a wild, romantic grove,
> Near many a hermit-fancied cove . . .
> An aged Judge, I saw him rove,
>   Dispensing good.

Arbigland House, Kirkbean, *c.* 1908. During one of his visits to this coastal estate about a dozen miles south of Dumfries Burns met Anna Benson, a lady who long after the poet's death described him in a letter to Jane Welsh Carlyle as 'incapable of rudeness or vulgarity . . . well bred and gentlemanly in all the courtesies of life'.

Blackwood House, Auldgirth, *c.* 1908. According to the inscription on this old postcard, Allan Cunningham was born (in 1784) in a cottage on this estate as the son of a gardener. Cunningham himself started out as a stonemason's apprentice, but later on he went to London where he eventually became a respected man of letters. In 1834 he issued *The Works of Robert Burns with his Life* in an edition of eight volumes.

The Murray Arms Hotel, Gatehouse-of-Fleet, *c.* 1960, where in 1793 Burns composed the song popularly known as 'Scots Wha Hae':

> Scots, wha hae wi' Wallace bled,
> Scots, wham Bruce has aften led,
> Welcome to your gory bed,
>   Or to Victorie! . . .

Looking from the railway station along Church Gate towards High Street, Moffat, 1940s, with the low-roofed Black Bull pictured on the right-hand side of the road. The Black Bull dates from the mid-sixteenth century and is one of Moffat's oldest buildings. For several years during the 'Killing Times' it was the headquarters of 'Bloody' Claverhouse while he hunted down the scores of Covenanters who took refuge in the surrounding hills. Burns was a frequent visitor to Moffat and he sometimes lodged at the Black Bull when travelling back and forth to Edinburgh. It was here, in 1793, that he composed his famous epigram on Miss Deborah Davies, which was inscribed on one of the Black Bull's window-panes:

> Ask why God made the gem so small?
> And why so huge the granite? –
> Because God meant mankind shoud set
> That higher value on it.

Miss Davies was a relation of the Riddell family who owned Friars' Carse, and Burns had made her acquaintance when living nearby at Ellisland. The poet once described her as 'positively the least creature ever I saw, to be at the same time unexceptionably, and indeed uncommonly, handsome and beautiful . . .'. The original window-pane with the epigram inscribed on it has long since disappeared but, at the beginning of 1996, a replica window bearing a facsimile of the lines was unveiled in the Black Bull's lounge by Murdo Morrison and John Inglis, President and Secretary respectively of the Burns Federation.

The Black Bull, Moffat, seen here probably much as it was in Burns's day. The inn is still a thriving concern popular with tourists and local residents, and an oval bronze plaque to be found on the rear wall officially confirms the Black Bull's status as a 'Burns Place of Interest'.

The Crook Inn, Tweedsmuir, 1940s. The external appearance of the building is little changed today. The Crook, set in the upper reaches of the Tweed valley, was Scotland's first licensed coaching inn and has been in existence since 1604. The seventeenth-century bar, still much used by locals, visitors and travellers along the scenic route between Moffat and Edinburgh, originally served as a kitchen and it was in this room, so legend has it, that Burns (who called at the Crook on his way to Edinburgh) wrote 'Sic a Wife as Willie had'. Needless to say the bar has been named after the hero of the piece. 'Willie Wastle'. Allan Cunningham tells that the heroine of this humorous satire was a farmer's wife who lived near Ellisland. As the Welsh poet W.H. Davies commented much later, it must have been a comfort to her descendants that her name did not survive.

> Willie Wastle dwalt on Tweed,
> The spot they ca'd it Linkumdoddie;
> Willie was a wabster gude,
> Could stown a clue wi' ony body:
> He had a wife was dour and din,
> O Tinkler Maidgie was her mither;
> Sic a wife as Willie had,
> I was na gie a button for her.
>
> She has an e'e, she has but ane,
> The cat has twa the very colour;
> Five rusty teeth, forbye a stump,
> A clapper tongue wad deave a miller;
> A whiskin beard about her mou,
> Her nose and chin they threaten ither;
> Sic a wife as Wille had,
> I wad na gie a button for her. . . .

CHAPTER EIGHT
THE IMMORTAL MEMORY

ROBERT BURNS.

The National Poet of Scotland was born at Alloway on the 25th of January.
1759. and died at Dumfries. July 21st. 1796.
He'll hae misfortunes great and sma'
But aye a heart aboon them a'
He'll be a credit till us a'
We'll a' be proud o' Robin.

The Burns Monument, Ayr, *c.* 1910. Situated in the town's Burns Statue Square, the memorial was unveiled on 11 July 1891. It comprises a bronze statue of the poet sculpted by George Lawson of London, with the figure standing on a pedestal into which are set panels illustrating scenes from some of Burns's most famous works, including 'Tam o' Shanter' and 'The Cottar's Saturday Night'. James A. Mackay, writing in *The Land o' Burns* (1996), mentions that casts of Lawson's statue have since been erected in Melbourne, Vancouver, Montreal and Winnipeg, with smaller versions to be seen in Ayr Old Church, Belfast Art Gallery and the Sorbonne, Paris.

'Kirkton Jean's' headstone in Kirkoswald churchyard, 1920s. Properly called Jean Kennedy, she kept an alehouse in the village with her sister Anne. The Revd James Muir, a former minister of Kirkoswald, explained that 'both sisters, because of their manners being somehow more than averagely refined, were known as 'the leddies' [ladies], and their humble hostelry as 'the leddies house'.' As a schoolboy at Kirkoswald, Burns must have been familiar with the premises and he recalled them (and 'Kirkton Jean') in 'Tam o' Shanter': 'That at the Lord's [leddies'] house e'en on Sunday/Thou drank with Kirkton Jean till Monday. . . .'

The headstone of John Davidson's grave in the churchyard at Kirkoswald. A shoemaker by trade, Davidson, who lived from 1728 to 1806, is widely believed to have been the prototype for the character of 'Souter Johnie' in 'Tam o' Shanter':

> . . . Ae market night,
> Tam had got planted unco right,
> Fast by an ingle, bleezing finely,
> Wi' reaming swats, that drank divinely;
> And at his elbow, 'Souter Johnie',
> His ancient, trusty, drouthy crony:
> Tam lo'ed him like a very brither. . . .

An undated view of Main Street, Kirkoswald (above) showing 'Souter Johnie's' house on the left. Below, the same house, where John Davidson lived from 1785 until his death in 1806, is pictured during the early 1900s. The thatched cottage is now open to the public as a museum containing Burnsiana and a shoemaker's workshop. Already familiar to us through 'Tam o' Shanter', we catch another glimpse (of a kind!) of 'Souter Johnie' in a poem by one Michelson Porteous and quoted by the Revd James Muir:

> A gash, wee, fodgel body,
> Stood on his shanks baith tight and steady,
> As gleg's a hawk, as teuch's a wuddy;
>   Had gabby skill
> To crack a joke, wi' wit aye ready,
>   Dot owre a gill.

The nineteenth-century Ayrshire sculptor James Thom created this group of stone figures which are on display in the garden of 'Souter Johnie's' cottage at Kirkoswald. The four statues are of characters drawn from 'Tam o' Shanter': 'Tam', 'Souter Johnie', the landlord and the landlord's wife. Thom's sculptures are well known on both sides of the Atlantic. He created many statues over the years of characters taken from Burns's work, of which this group (frequently featured on tourist postcards and drawn from what is arguably Burns's finest poem) is probably the most famous.

The churchyard at Glenbervie (south-west of Stonehaven) in Kincardineshire, *c.* 1905, showing the tombstones of Burns's ancestors. Burns was descended from a line of tenant-farmers who had occupied various properties in this north-eastern part of the country. By a strange coincidence, it was also the region which produced one of Scotland's most respected twentieth-century writers, Lewis Grassic Gibbon (James Leslie Mitchell), who was born at Auchterless in 1901 and brought up in the Howe of the Mearns. His trilogy *A Scots Quair*, published between 1932 and 1934, has long been regarded as a classic work of modern Scottish literature.

The Burns Monument and Statue in Kay Park, Kilmarnock, 1920s. The foundation stone was laid on 14 September 1878, and the unveiling ceremony was carried out the following August by Colonel Alexander of Ballochmyle. There can be few – if perhaps any – other poets who have been so well represented as Burns is by statues and monuments placed in towns and cities around the world.

The Burns Monument, Alloway. Unveiled on 4 July 1823, the Grecian-style memorial was designed by Thomas Hamilton and built at a cost of just under £3,500. The surrounding gardens contain statues of 'Tam o' Shanter' and 'Souter Johnie' sculpted out of stone by James Thom.

The Hole I' The Wa' Inn's Burns Museum, Dumfries, late nineteenth century. John Thomson, the proprietor of the inn at that time, amassed an impressive collection of Burnsiana that was displayed in the bar, including the poet's Excise swordstick, his Dumfries Burgess ticket, his teapot and caddy, walking sticks, a Masonic jug, his toddy and punch ladles, letters, autographed manuscripts and even the poet's kitchen table.

The Burns National Memorial and Cottage Homes, Mauchline. The 67 ft high tower, built of red sandstone and divided into three floors, stands at the junction of the A76 and the road to Mossgiel adjacent to the lands of Burns's former home, and it affords a panoramic view over the surrounding countryside. Opened in May 1898, the Gothic-style tower houses, among other things, a number of Burns relics and the almost obligatory audio-visual display. The attractive cottages have traditionally been occupied by elderly people who are allowed to live in them rent-free.

The Tam o' Shanter Inn, High Street, Ayr, 1920s, which for some years housed a Burns museum. A painting over the doorway depicts 'Tam' mounting his grey mare Meg before setting out on his famous journey. 'Tam o' Shanter' and his creator are recalled annually in Ayr with a 'Burns Ride', a procession that follows the route taken by 'Tam' in the poem.

A Burns chair, one of the relics to be found at the Tam o' Shanter Inn when it housed a museum of Burnsiana. The premises served as an inn during the late eighteenth century and also from the mid-nineteenth to the mid-twentieth century. However, between 1957 and 1988 they were occupied by a museum devoted to the poet. After being closed for a while the building subsequently reopened as a public house, in which capacity it now serves tourists and the townspeople of Ayr.

Chair made from wood which composed the Printing Press on which the First Edition of Burns' Poems was printed.

This chair was made from wood that had originally formed part of the press used to print the first edition of Burns's *Poems, Chiefly in the Scottish Dialect* at Kilmarnock in 1786. 'One cannot help deprecating the vandalism', wrote James A. Mackay in his *Burnsiana* (1988), 'that destroyed a piece of machinery which would have been of unparalleled interest to Burns bibliophiles and scholars.' The chair was made in about 1858 and bears carvings representing 'The Twa Dogs', 'Tam' and 'Souter Johnie', and scenes that include the Auld Brig o' Doon. Completing what is a distinctly odd act of homage to the poet, a bust of Burns presides over the whole affair.

An interior view of Burns House, Dumfries. The house, which has been restored to preserve much of its flavour from the poet's time, attracts visitors from around the world. Among the many items of interest on display here are the chair in which Burns wrote his last poems and the gun that he carried when on duty as an Exciseman. Original letters and manuscripts can also be found here, together with the Kilmarnock and Edinburgh editions of his work.

Members of Dumfries Town Council placing a wreath on the poet's grave at the Burns Mausoleum in St Michael's churchyard, 1920s, as a part of the events held annually on 25 January to mark Burns's birthday.

The Burns Mausoleum, Dumfries, seen here before 1936. Originally Burns was buried in a simple grave nearby but, in September 1817, twenty-one years after his death, the poet's remains were transferred to this Grecian temple-style building whose appearance is certainly an acquired taste. Not only Burns himself but also his widow Jean and five members of their family are entombed in the Mausoleum. The foundation stone of this striking monument (designed by Thomas Hunt of London) was laid in June 1815, and the work took two years to complete. As the poet's final resting-place, the Mausoleum is an essential port of call for anyone following the town's 'Burns Trail'.

The Mausoleum, after 1936. In the top photograph Burns is seen standing behind the plough, whereas here the poet has clearly moved in front of that implement. The reason for the change is quite simple. The wet and windy climate of south-west Scotland took its toll on the original marble statuary, which was sculpted by Peter Turnerelli and installed at the time of the Mausoleum's completion. In 1936 the decayed figures were redone – again in marble – by Hermon Cawthra, who made some minor alterations to the original group in the process.

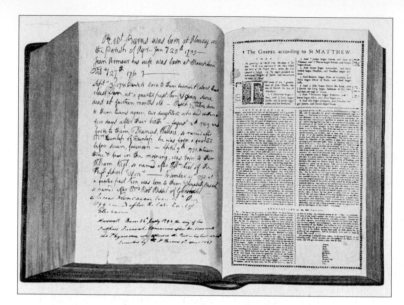

A reduced facsimile of Burns's Bible. Several Bibles that had some connection with the poet have survived, including the Armour Family Bible and 'Highland Mary's' Bible. The inscription seen here on the left-hand page of the poet's Family Bible is in Burns's own handwriting and records not only the details of his own birth but those of his wife and their first seven children as well. The final entry gives the details of Maxwell's birth, which occurred on the day of his father's funeral.

A postcard issued in 1959 on the bicentenary of Burns's birth, showing the poet himself in the centre, surrounded by people and places associated with his life and depicting characters from his work.

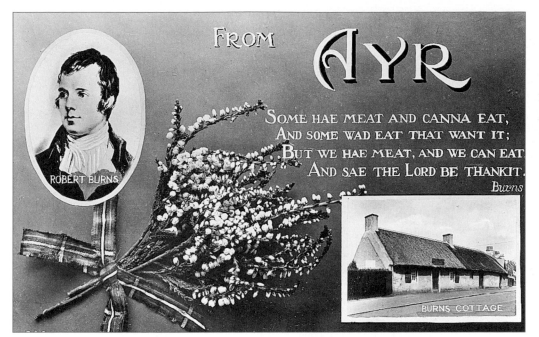

The life and work of Burns has given rise to a vast and still-thriving market in related tourist postcards. Only a few years ago the noted Burnsian Peter Westwood produced a definitive account of the subject in his *Deltiology of Robert Burns*. The example pictured here dates from between the wars and is typical of the genre, sporting as it does all the essential ingredients: a portrait of the man himself, a picture of his birthplace, a sprig of heather and the 'Selkirk Grace'.

A postcard reflecting the universal and enduring appeal of Burns and his work.

The 150th Anniversary of the Birth
1759 :: of :: Robert Burns 1909

Should auld acquaintance be forgot,
And never brought to min'?
Should auld acquaintance be forgot,
And days o' lang syne?

A postcard sporting the famous Nasmyth portrait of Burns, and issued in 1909 to mark the 150th anniversary of the poet's birth.

The Nasmyth portrait of Burns has been reproduced *ad nauseam* over the years, emblazoned on anything from postcards and pub signs to teaspoons and boxes of shortbread. In what might be considered another unusual act of homage to her illustrious forbear, the poet's great-granddaughter Miss Jean Armour Burns Brown (who was descended through Burns's eldest son) made herself the subject of this portrait, decked out in the style of the Nasmyth Burns. The similar hair-do and attire emphasize what was undoubtedly a remarkable case of hereditary likeness. She was the last surviving descendant of Burns to live in Dumfries and died in 1937.

THE NATIONAL COMMEMORATION
OF THE
CENTENARY OF THE DEATH OF ROBERT BURNS,
TUESDAY, 21st JULY, 1896.

PLAN showing Route of Procession for Public Bodies, Burns Clubs, Freemasons, Trades, Societies, &c., &c.   For Particulars see other side.

A plan showing the route taken through Dumfries by the procession to mark the centenary of Burns's death that was held on 21 July 1896. Members drawn from Burns Clubs throughout the United Kingdom attended the event, and delegates representing Burns Clubs in the USA, Canada, Australia and New Zealand were also among those who gathered in the town for the occasion.

Menu.

"Some hae meat and canna eat,
And some wad eat that want it;
But we hae meat, and we can eat,
And sae the Lord be thankit."

HARE SOUP.   COCKIE-LEEKIE.

"A toothfu' tae redd the road."

HOWFF SCOTCH HAGGIS.

"Great Chieftain o' the Puddin' race,
Aboon them a' ye tak' your place."

SHEEPHEAD AND TROTTERS.

"What though on hamely fare we dine."

ROAST BEEF.   ROAST GOOSE.
STEWED TURKEY.

"Oiled by a wee drap,
The wheels o' life gae doon-hill scrievin."

POTATOES.
MASHED NEEPS AND GREENS.

"Anither drappie o' the 'Tappit Hen.'"

BEEFSTEAK PIE.   RABBIT PIE.
COLD FOWL.

"Food fills the wame, and keeps us leevin'."

PLUM PUDDING.   APPLE TART.
FRUIT.

"O Lord, since we have feasted thus,
Which we so little merit,
Let Meg now take away the flesh,
And Jock bring in the spirit."

The menu (left) and the toast list (below) for the Dumfries Burns Howff Club Supper held at the Globe, Dumfries (the club's regular meeting place) on 26 January 1925, under the chairmanship of George Hastings. Among those who attended the occasion were G.W. Shirley and J.W. Howat (representing Dumfries Burns Club), S. Baker and D. Byers (representing the Queensberry Club), and National Union of Railwaymen officials C.T. Cramp and J. Marchbank. Of course, Burns Suppers are held annually around the world to mark the poet's birthday and to honour his name and fame. This Supper held at the poet's favourite 'howff' is at

Toast List.

"A towmond o' trouble, should that be my fa',
A night o' gude fellowship sowthers it a'."

"King, Queen, and Royal Family" ... ... Chairman.
National Anthem.

"The Imperial Forces" ... ... Chairman.
"Rule, Britannia."

Song—"Scots wha hae" ... ... Mr F. M'Murdo.

Greetings from other Clubs ... ... Secretary.

"THE IMMORTAL MEMORY," W. J. HAY, Esq., Edinburgh.
"He'll be a credit till us a—
We'll a' be proud o' Robin !"

Song—"There was a Lad" ... ... Mr W. Pearson.

Recitation—"Epistle to Davie" ... ... Mr P. W. Smith.

"Kindred Clubs" ... ... Mr J. W. Howat.
"Hale be your heart, hale be your fiddle !
Lang may your elbuck jink and diddle."

Song—"To Mary in Heaven" ... ... Mr A. Love.
Reply—Deputations.

Song—"Ca' the Yowes to the Knowes" ... ... Mr A. Doyle.

"Our Guest" ... ... Chairman.
"May couthie Fortune, kind and cannie, be thy lot."

Trio—"Willie Brewed" ... Messrs Logue, M'Murdo, and Pearson.

"The Lassies" ... ... Mr P. W. Smith.
"A man may kiss a bonnie lass
And ay be welcome back again."

Song—"Green Grow the Rashes" ... ... Mr J. Maxwell.
Reply—Mr W. Wilson.

Song—"The Lea-Rig" ... ... Mr W. Logue.

"The Hostess" ... ... Mr T. Laidlaw.
"For sense and good taste she will vie wi' the best."

Song—"The Lass o' Ballochmyle" ... ... Mr W. Wilson.
Reply—Mr John Grierson.

"The Chairman" ... ... Croupiers.

"Croupiers" ... ... Chairman.
"Auld Lang Syne."

Accompanist—Mr A. M'George.   Piper—Mr W. Kirkpatrick.

The toast list for the evening. All the usual loyal and patriotic toasts were pledged on this occasion: to the bard's immortal memory; to the guest for the evening (W.J. Hay of Edinburgh); to the lassies and the hostess, etc. The local newspaper reported that the haggis was piped in by Mr W. Kirkpatrick, and that 'from start to finish the gathering was a real homely and thoroughly enjoyable affair'.

Wreaths being laid at the Burns Statue in Dumfries, during celebrations held in January 1959 to mark the bicentenary of the poet's birth. Among those gathered here are Hugh Cunningham, Ernie Robertson and George McKerrow. The ceremony was held during the morning, followed by a concert at the town's Lyceum Cinema in the evening at which, according to a report in the local newspaper, 'the programme was sustained by the Band of the 5th King's Own Scottish Borderers, local orchestras, choirs and dancing teams'. Among the celebrities who attended bicentenary events in Dumfries were the writer A.P. Herbert and the actor James Robertson Justice.

The Burns Statue, Dumfries, *c.* 1920. This more than life-size figure of the poet, worked in Carrara marble and designed by Amelia Hill, was financed by public subscription and unveiled by the Earl of Rosebery on 6 April 1882. Over the years the position of the memorial has been slightly altered to make way for road improvements, but its present site, in the shadow of Greyfriars' Church and commanding a view of the High Street, is testimony to the unique place that Burns occupies in the life and history of the town. The iron railings seen here were removed during the Second World War.

TAM LO'ED HIM LIKE A VERA BRITHER.

A pageant depicting the life and work of Burns was presented in a series of tableaux (above and below) at the Royal Highland Show, Park Farm, Dumfries, in June 1954. The tableaux, organized by the Thornhill Show Sports Committee and Holywood Young Farmers' Club, were mounted on lorries and formed part of an afternoon parade around the showground. Scenes from Burns's most famous poems were represented, including 'Tam o' Shanter' (above) and 'The Cottar's Saturday Night' (below). Those taking part in the latter included John Henderson, Ian Marchbank, Jean McGeorge, Margaret Carmichael, Shirley Adamson and Daisy Adamson. The Queen Mother attended the show and, according to the local newspaper, she 'was particularly amused by several unrehearsed incidents which occurred during the tableaux parade. The lorry depicting "We twa hae paidl't in the burn" stuck in the mud in front of the Royal Box, and the crowd cheered lustily when the Duke of Buccleuch and other members of the Drumlanrig house party rushed to the back of the lorry and pushed with all their strength. . . . A minute or two later the same scene had to be enacted as a lorry carrying a tableau depicting "To a Louse" also got stuck in the mud.'

FROM SCENES LIKE THESE AULD SCOTIA'S GRANDEUR SPRIN

That Sacred hour can I forget,
Can I forget the hallowed Grove,
Where by the winding Ayr we met
To live one day of parting love.
—Burns.

Failfrod, Tarbolton, where Burns parted with Highland Mary

Failford, west of Mauchline. A red sandstone monument was built here in 1921 close to the supposed spot where Burns and 'Highland Mary' parted in 1786.

> That sacred hour can I forget,
> Can I forget the hallowed grove,
> Where by the winding Ayr we met
> To live one day of parting love.

Waterfoot, Annan, c. 1950. There was a time when this was the main port area of the town, boasting an inn, warehousing, wooden piers and other facilities connected to Annan's once-famous fishing industry. As such the locality was well known to Burns the Exciseman. In June 1997 a commemorative cairn dedicated to the poet was unveiled here by Edith Graham-Barnett who, at the time, was the oldest member of the Solway Burns Club of Annan.

A close-up view of Peter Turnerelli's marble creation in the Burns Mausoleum. Representing the Muse of Poetry presiding over Burns at the plough, the sculpture has at times proved as controversial as the Mausoleum itself, having both its admirers and detractors. This photograph was taken before 1936 and shows Turnerelli's original work, with Burns standing behind the plough. After its removal from the Mausoleum, the statue of the poet was displayed for a time in Burns House nearby. Eventually, however, it turned up in a local builder's yard and has subsequently been lost. Great would be the rejoicing were the figure ever to surface again.

ACKNOWLEDGEMENTS

I am grateful to the following for providing photographs and background information:

Ian Ball, Mrs C. Barbour, *Dumfries & Galloway Standard*, Elizabeth Edwards, Dave Smith (Hon. Sec., the Burns Howff Club, Dumfries), Ernie Smith, Morag Williams (Archivist, Dumfries & Galloway Health Board). Photographs on the following pages appear with the permission of Richard Stenlake: 4, 15 (bottom), 20 (bottom), 22, 25, 26 (bottom), 27 (bottom), 28 (bottom), 30 (bottom), 31, 32 (bottom), 36 (top), 37, 38 (top), 47, 50 (top), 61 (top), 68, 71 (bottom), 72, 74 (bottom), 82, 84, 88, 90 (bottom), 91 (top), 95 (top), 97, 98 (bottom), 99, 100, 101 (bottom), 103, 111, 112 (bottom), 113, 114 (bottom), 117 (bottom), 124 (top). Photographs on pages 15 (top), 16 (top), 17, 18 (top), 90 (top) and 149 (top) appear with the permission of Denholm T. Reid.

BIBLIOGRAPHY

I consulted many sources while preparing this volume. However, the following titles proved indispensable:

Boyle, A.M. *The Ayrshire Book of Burns-Lore*, Ayr, Alloway Publishing Ltd, 1996 edn
Davies, W.H. (ed.), *The Poetical Works of Burns*. London, Collins, undated
Lindsay, Maurice. *The Burns Encyclopedia*, London, Robert Hale, 1980 edn
Mackay, James A. *Burns-Lore of Dumfries and Galloway*, Ayr, Alloway Publishing Ltd, 1988
——, *Burnsiana*, Ayr, Alloway Publishing Ltd, 1988
——, *The Land o' Burns*, HMSO Edinburgh, 1996

Other titles published by The History Press

The Landscape of Scotland: A Hidden History

From lochs, coastlines and waterways, to highlands, forests and fields, this book examines how the lie of the Scottish land holds countless archaeological sites both above and below ground: farmsteads, castles, standing stones and many more.

978-0-7524-1484-3

Glasgow

Bearing a rich history and proud traditions, in the nineteenth century Scotland generated vast wealth through commerce, manufacturing and heavy industry which made Glasgow the 'Second City of the Empire' and shipbuilder to the world. This book reflects the character of the hardworking population whose chequered lives have created the modern city of Glasgow.

978-0-7524-4962-3

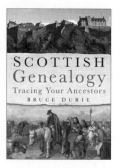

Scottish Genealogy

Scotland has possibly the most complete and best-kept set of records and other documents in the world. Given both this and the extraordinary worldwide Scottish diaspora (approximately 28 million people can claim Scottish ancestry), the lack of a thorough guide to Scottish genealogy is a significant gap. Bruce Durie's book bridges that gap with authority and provides a sense of the excitement of the historical chase.

978-0-7509-4568-4

Scotland: From Prehistory to Present

From the early settlers after the last Ice Age, and the myth and ritual that surrounds that prehistoric period, Fiona Watson charts the evolution of the Scottish people – as Scots, Picts and Angles – and their interaction with the world abroad, from invasions by the Romans and Vikings and the medieval wars of independence with England right through to Devolution.

978-0-7524-2591-7

Visit our website and discover thousands of other History Press books.

www.thehistorypress.co.uk